Sage
explaine

OTHER TITLES OF INTEREST

Sage
explained

by

D. Weale

BERNARD BABANI (publishing) LTD
THE GRAMPIANS
SHEPHERDS BUSH ROAD
LONDON W6 7NF
ENGLAND

PLEASE NOTE

Although every care has been taken with the production of this book to ensure that any instructions or any of the other contents operate in a correct and safe manner, the Author and the Publishers do not accept any responsibility for any failure, damage or loss caused by following the said contents. The Author and Publisher do not take any responsibility for errors or omissions.

The Author and Publisher shall not be liable to the purchaser or to any other person or legal entity with respect to any liability, loss or damage caused or alleged to be caused directly or indirectly by this book. The book is sold as is, without any warranty of any kind, either expressed or implied, respecting the contents, including but not limited to implied warranties regarding the book's quality, performance, correctness or fitness for any particular purpose.

No part of this book may be reproduced or copied by any means whatever without written permission of the Publisher.

© 1993 BERNARD BABANI (publishing) LTD

First published May 1993
Reprinted – September 1994
Reprinted – February 1996

British Library Cataloguing in Publication Data

Weale, D.
SAGE Explained
I. Title
657.02855369
ISBN 0 85934 328 6

TRADEMARKS

MS-DOS is the registered trademark of Microsoft Corporation

SAGE Bookkeeper, Accountant, Accountant Plus, Financial Controller and Payroll are registered trademarks of the SAGE GROUP PLC.

Printed and bound in Great Britain
by Cox & Wyman Ltd, Reading, Berkshire

ABOUT THE AUTHOR

David Weale is a Fellow of the Institute of Chartered Accountants and has worked in both private and public practice. At present he is a lecturer in business computing at Yeovil College.

Apart from computing his interests are cycling and running.

He lives in Somerset with his wife, three children and Siamese cat.

DEDICATION

This book is dedicated to my long-suffering wife.

Table of Contents

INTRODUCTION

Hi, this book is intended to be an explanation of the SAGE suite of accounting programs. It is not intended to replace the manuals that come with the program but to offer an alternative explanation of the program.

The book is aimed at anyone who needs the concepts explained in simple terms, anyone who wants a summary of what the program is capable of achieving (possibly before purchasing it) and any firm who need additional texts for all their users of SAGE.

All the aspects of SAGE Financial Controller 5 (including the Stock option) and Payroll 2 are covered so that anyone who has any of the SAGE programs can make good use of the book.

D. Weale

USEFUL INFORMATION

How SAGE is Organised

The program is menu driven, this means that you will be presented with a series of menus (choices). You choose the activity you want from each and then you will be presented with other menus and so on until you reach the screen you want.

The basic organisation is shown in a diagram below (this is not a complete picture of every menu but is an indication of the way in which the menus are structured).

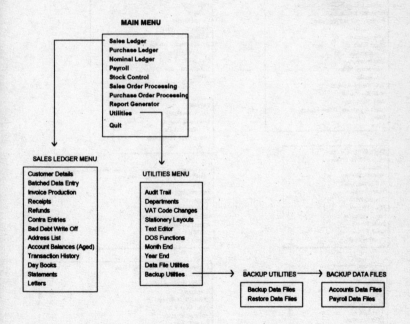

The full menu structure is shown below

SAGE MENU LAYOUT

Main Menu
Sales Ledger
Purchase Ledger
Nominal Ledger
Payroll
Stock Control
Sales Order Processing
Purchase Order Processing
Report Generator
Utilities

Sales Ledger Menu
Customer Details
Batched Data Entry
Invoice Production
Receipts
Refunds
Contra Entries
Bad Debts Write Off
Address List
Account Balances (Aged)
Transaction History
Day Books
Statements
Letters

Nominal Ledger Menu
Nominal Account Structure
Bank Transactions
Petty Cash Transactions
Journal Entries
Recurring Entries
Prepayments and Accruals
Depreciation
Consolidation
Quick Ratio
Accounts List
Trail Balance
Transaction History
Day Books
VAT Return Analysis
Bank Reconciliation
Bank Statement
Profit & Loss and Balance Sheet
Budget Report
Asset Valuation

Purchase Ledger Menu
Supplier Details
Batched Data Entry
Payments
Refunds
Contra Entries
Write Off Account
Address List
Account Balances (Aged)
Transaction History
Day Books
Remittance Advice Notes
Letters

Payroll
Employee Details
Processing Payroll
Statutory Sick Pay
Government Parameters
Company Details

Stock Control Menu
Update Stock Details
Categories
Adjustments In
Adjustments Out
Stock Transfers
Stock Details
Stock History
Stock Valuation
Profit Report
Stock Explosion
Re-order Levels

Sales Order Processing Menu
Enter Stock Orders
Process Stock Orders
Enquiries
Order Status Reports
Order Acknowledgements
Amend Despatches
Create Invoice Details
Delete Orders

Utilities Menu
Audit Trail
Departments
VAT Code Changes
Stationery Layouts
Text Editors
DOS Functions
Month End
Year End
Control Accounts
Global Changes
Posting Error Corrections
Incomplete Transactions
Data File Changes
Data Verification
File Import
Backup Utilities
Defaults

Purchase Order Processing Menu
Enter Purchase Orders
Process Purchase Orders
Enquiries
Order Status Reports
Order Documents
Amend Deliveries
Delete Orders

Report Generator
Sales Ledger
Purchase Ledger
Nominal Ledger
Management Reports
Payroll
Invoice Production
Stock Control
Sales Order Processing
Purchase Order Processing

4

Useful Keys

The following diagram lists the useful keys that are used within SAGE. It is worthwhile committing these to memory or photocopying this page for reference (though not all these keys work with all options).

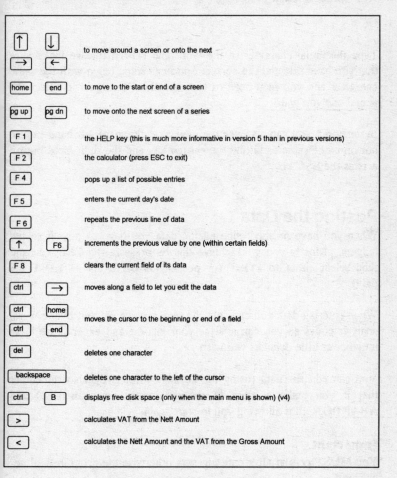

↑ ↓		to move around a screen or onto the next
→ ←		
home end		to move to the start or end of a screen
pg up pg dn		to move onto the next screen of a series
F 1		the HELP key (this is much more informative in version 5 than in previous versions)
F 2		the calculator (press ESC to exit)
F 4		pops up a list of possible entries
F 5		enters the current day's date
F 6		repeats the previous line of data
↑	F6	increments the previous value by one (within certain fields)
F 8		clears the current field of its data
ctrl	→	moves along a field to let you edit the data
ctrl	home	moves the cursor to the beginning or end of a field
ctrl	end	
del		deletes one character
backspace		deletes one character to the left of the cursor
ctrl	B	displays free disk space (only when the main menu is shown) (v4)
>		calculates VAT from the Nett Amount
<		calculates the Nett Amount and the VAT from the Gross Amount

In version 5 of SAGE there is a display of some of the useful function keys at the bottom of most screens.

How to Select Options Within a Menu

You have several choices here. Either:

Move the cursor onto the option required and **return**

Or

Type the initial character of the word and **return** (please make sure that you have selected the correct option as some begin with the same character and you may need to type the character again to select the actual one you want).

In version 5 you can also use the mouse, clicking the left hand mouse button is the same as hitting the **return** key and the right hand button acts as the **ESC** key.

Posting the Data

When you have finished entering the data you have to post it to the ledgers. Mostly you will achieve this by pressing the **ESC** key and then select either to **POST** (or possibly **ABANDON** or **EDIT** the data).

When entering data you can split the total invoice amount over several analysis codes so you can analyse your income and expenditure in as much or as little detail as you wish.

You can edit the data (using the keys shown above), also remember that if you make a mess of the data entry you can **ESC** and **ABANDON**, thus allowing you to start again.

Important

You MUST **return** after entering data otherwise the program will not accept it.

ALWAYS check the data you have entered **BEFORE** posting it.

Using the Calculator

You can use the calculator **(F2)** to work out sums, the answer will then automatically appear in the relevant part of the data entry screen (for example you can do the calculation using the SAGE calculator and if you **return** after working out the answer, it will appear at the cursor position on the screen). This avoids mistakes that can be made copying figures from a hand held calculator or by working out the calculation in your head.

Initially

When SAGE is loaded, you will be presented with a screen identifying the program and then the next screen will be shown, this asks for the date and password.

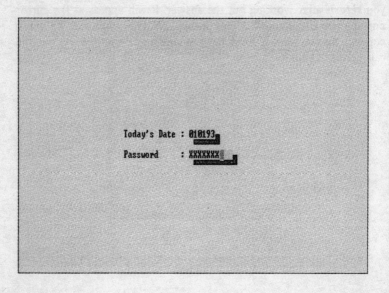

Today's Date

The date you want to use for the session, this does not have to be the current date, but may be any date you wish e.g. 010193 (to enter the opening balances for the year). The date has to be entered as a six digit number (no spaces) followed by the **return** key.

Password

The default password is **LETMEIN** (followed by the **return** key). You can alter this if you wish (see appendix three).

The actual password is not shown for security reasons.

STARTING SAGE

Once the date and password have been entered, the Main menu is displayed. This shows the options available within the program.

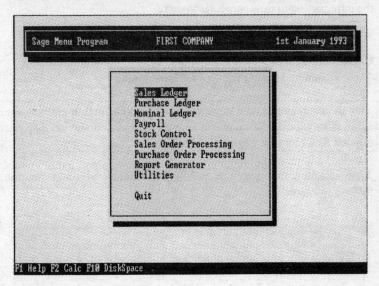

```
 Sage Menu Program        FIRST COMPANY        1st January 1993

                    ┌──────────────────────────┐
                    │ Sales Ledger             │
                    │ Purchase Ledger          │
                    │ Nominal Ledger           │
                    │ Payroll                  │
                    │ Stock Control            │
                    │ Sales Order Processing   │
                    │ Purchase Order Processing│
                    │ Report Generator         │
                    │ Utilities                │
                    │                          │
                    │ Quit                     │
                    └──────────────────────────┘

 F1 Help F2 Calc F10 DiskSpace
```

Setting Up SAGE

Before you can use any accounting program, you must set it for your business. The obvious parameters that will need entering are:

* Customers' or clients' names and addresses
* Suppliers' names and addresses
* Account codes

You will also need to enter the opening balances (the balances that exist when the computerised records begin).

> Always begin your computerised accounts at the start of a month, not part way through a month.

I would suggest that when you use a computerised system for the first time that you continue to operate the manual system (how long you do this is up to you and your accountant) and to check one against the other. This is called parallel running and is a standard procedure for the introduction of new computer systems.

Customer Names and Addresses

These are entered using the **Sales Ledger** option.

> You should organise your customer list into order before entering the data. Also allocate the customer references in such a way so that you can add new customers easily.

After selecting this option from the Main menu, you will see the following screen:

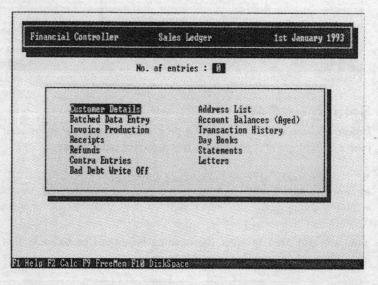

To enter or alter the customer names or addresses choose the **Customer Details** option, the data entry screen will appear:

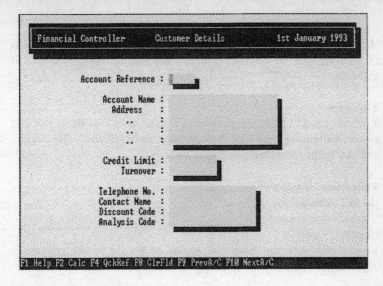

```
              Account Reference :

                  Account Name :
                       Address :
                            .. :
                            .. :
                            .. :

                  Credit Limit :
                      Turnover :

                 Telephone No. :
                  Contact Name :
                 Discount Code :
                 Analysis Code :
```

F1 Help F2 Calc F4 QckRef F8 ClrFld F9 PrevA/C F10 NextA/C

The data to be entered is:

Account Reference

This is a six digit reference which you allocate to each of your customers, numbers can be used as well as letters, the important things to remember are:

*   choose easy to remember codes
*   short codes are quicker to type

The code is used to retrieve customer details from the files so it is impossible to use the same code for different customers. After entering a new code you will be asked if this is a new customer and then you can enter the rest of the details.

Account Name and Address

Each line can be up to 25 characters in length, remember to **return** after each line (including the last), otherwise it will not be accepted. It may be that the name or address will not fit conveniently into the space in which case you will have to abbreviate it, it is best to leave the last line purely for the postcode though.

11

Credit Limit

Here you enter a credit limit (if you wish), this is used in certain parts of the program to display warning messages if the credit limit is exceeded.

Turnover

You only need to enter the cumulative figure (so far) for the year if you are computerising part way through your financial year. This figure will change to reflect the cumulative turnover.

Telephone Number

Up to 15 characters

Contact Name

Very useful, you can enter the names of people in the customer's organisation you normally speak to (up to 20 characters).

Discount Code

This is tied into the Stock Control system and you can enter any of the following:

A
B
C
Dnn   (nn being a percentage discount, e.g. D20 means 20%)

The values for A, B and C are discount rates you have (or are going to) set up in the Stock system. D is a special discount rate which you can apply to individual customers so that you have complete flexibility within your discount structure.

Analysis Code

This is used in conjunction with the Report Generator to allow you to sort and select data. Up to 16 characters can be used, e.g. you may wish to analyse the customers by geographical area (perhaps by entering a town name or postcode).

When all the data has been entered, **ESC** and **POST** the details. If you have made mistakes or wish to alter the record choose **EDIT** or **ABANDON**.

Suppliers' Details

These are entered in exactly the same way as the customers, choose **Purchase Ledger** and then **Supplier Details**.

Account Codes

These are codes you allocate to different types of income and expenditure, SAGE has a set of default codes which you can use, alter, delete or ignore as you wish. The codes are grouped depending upon where they appear in the accounts.

The Default Codes

These individual codes are automatically set up by the program (assuming you accept the default settings). They can be added to or altered as you wish or deleted if you want to reduce the number of codes.

0010	FREEHOLD PROPERTY	0011	LEASEHOLD PROPERTY
0020	PLANT AND MACHINERY	0021	P/M DEPRECIATION
0030	OFFICE EQUIPMENT	0031	O/E DEPRECIATION
0040	FURNITURE AND FIXTURES	0041	F/F DEPRECIATION
0050	MOTOR VEHICLES	0051	M/V DEPRECIATION
1001	STOCK	1002	WORK IN PROGRESS
1003	FINISHED GOODS	1100	DEBTORS CONTROL ACCOUNT
1101	SUNDRY DEBTORS	1102	OTHER DEBTORS
1103	PREPAYMENTS	1200	BANK CURRENT ACCOUNT
1210	BANK DEPOSIT ACCOUNT	1220	BUILDING SOCIETY ACCOUNT
1230	PETTY CASH	2100	CREDITORS CONTROL ACCOUNT
2101	SUNDRY CREDITORS	2102	OTHER CREDITORS
2109	ACCRUALS	2200	TAX CONTROL ACCOUNT
2201	VAT LIABILITY	2210	P.A.Y.E.
2211	NATIONAL INSURANCE	2230	PENSION FUND
2300	LOANS	2310	HIRE PURCHASE
2320	CORPORATION TAX	2330	MORTGAGES
3000	ORDINANCE SHARES	3001	PREFERENCE SHARES
3100	RESERVES	3101	UNDISTRIBUTED RESERVES
3200	PROFIT AND LOSS ACCOUNT	4000	SALES TYPE A
4001	SALES TYPE B	4002	SALES TYPE C
4009	DISCOUNTS ALLOWED	4100	SALES TYPE D
4101	SALES TYPE E	4200	SALES OF ASSETS
4900	MISCELLANEOUS INCOME	4901	ROYALTIES RECEIVED
4902	COMMISSIONS RECEIVED	4903	INSURANCE CLAIMS
4904	RENT INCOME	4905	DISTRIBUTION AND CARRIAGE
5000	MATERIALS PURCHASES	5001	MATERIALS IMPORTED
5002	MISCELLANEOUS PURCHASES	5003	PACKAGING
5009	DISCOUNTS TAKEN	5100	CARRIAGE
5101	DUTY	5102	TRANSPORT INSURANCE
5200	OPENING STOCK	5201	CLOSING STOCK
6000	PRODUCTIVE LABOUR	6001	COST OF SALES LABOUR
6002	SUB-CONTRACTORS	6100	SALES COMMISSIONS
6200	SALES PROMOTIONS	6201	ADVERTISING
6202	GIFTS AND SAMPLES	6203	P.R. (LIT. & BROCHURES)
6900	MISCELLANEOUS EXPENSES	7001	DIRECTORS SALARIES
7002	DIRECTORS REMUNERATION	7003	STAFF SALARIES
7004	WAGES - REGULAR	7005	WAGES - CASUAL
7006	EMPLOYERS N.I.	7007	EMPLOYERS PENSIONS

7008	RECRUITMENT EXPENSES	7100	RENT
7102	WATER RATES	7103	GENERAL RATES
7104	PREMISES INSURANCE	7200	ELECTRICITY
7201	GAS	7202	OIL
7203	OTHER HEATING COSTS	7300	FUEL AND OIL
7301	REPAIRS AND SERVICING	7302	LICENCES
7303	VEHICLE INSURANCE	7304	MISC. MOTOR EXPENSES
7400	TRAVELLING	7401	CAR HIRE
7402	HOTELS	7403	U.K. ENTERTAINMENT
7404	OVERSEAS ENTERTAINMENT	7405	OVERSEAS TRAVELLING
7406	SUBSISTENCE	7500	PRINTING
7501	POSTAGE AND CARRIAGE	7502	TELEPHONE
7503	TELEX/TELEGRAM/FACSIMILE	7504	OFFICE STATIONERY
7505	BOOKS ETC.	7600	LEGAL FEES
7601	AUDIT & ACCOUNTANCY FEES	7602	CONSULTANCY FEES
7603	PROFESSIONAL FEES	7700	EQUIPMENT HIRE
7701	OFFICE MACHINE MAINT.	7800	REPAIRS AND RENEWALS
7801	CLEANING	7802	LAUNDRY
7803	PREMISES EXPENSES (MICS)	7900	BANK INTEREST PAID
7901	BANK CHARGES	7902	CURRENCY CHARGES
7903	LOAN INTEREST PAID	7904	H.P. INTEREST
7905	CREDIT CHARGES	8000	DEPRECIATION
8001	PLANT & MACHINERY DEPR.	8002	FURNITURE/FIX/FITTINGS DP
8003	VEHICLE DEPRECIATION	8004	OFFICE EQUIPMENT DEPR.
8100	BAD DEBT WRITE OFF	8102	BAD DEBT PROVISION
8200	DONATIONS	8201	SUBSCRIPTIONS
8202	CLOTHING COSTS	8203	TRAINING COSTS
8204	INSURANCE	8205	REFRESHMENTS
9998	SUSPENSE ACCOUNT	9999	MISPOSTINGS ACCOUNT

Codes Listed By Group

These are the codes shown above but allocated into groups. The groups are organised by heading and appear in the Trading, Profit And Loss Account and Balance Sheet. Again these can be altered and are shown on the next page.

Profit And Loss Account groups

Sales

PRODUCT SALES	4000	4099
EXPORT SALES	4100	4199
SALES OF ASSETS	4200	4299
OTHER SALES	4900	4999

Purchases

PURCHASES	5000	5099
PURCHASE CHARGES	5100	5199
STOCK	5200	5299

Direct Expenses

LABOUR	6000	6099
COMMISSIONS	6100	6199
MISCELLANEOUS EXPENSES	6900	6999
SALES PROMOTION	6200	6299

Overheads

SALARIES AND WAGES	7000	7099
RENT AND RATES	7100	7199
HEAT, LIGHT AND POWER	7200	7299
MOTOR EXPENSES	7300	7399
TRAVELLING AND ENTERTAINMENT	7400	7499
PRINTING AND STATIONERY	7500	7599
PROFESSIONAL FEES	7600	7699
EQUIPMENT HIRE AND RENTAL	7700	7799
MAINTENANCE	7800	7899
BANK CHARGES AND INTEREST	7900	7999
DEPRECIATION	8000	8099
BAD DEBTS	8100	8199
GENERAL EXPENSES	8200	8299

Balance Sheet groups

Fixed Assets

PROPERTY	0010	0019
PLANT AND MACHINERY	0020	0029
OFFICE EQUIPMENT	0030	0039
FURNITURE AND FIXTURES	0040	0049
MOTOR VEHICLES	0050	0059

Current Assets

STOCK	1000	1099
DEBTORS	1100	1199
DEPOSITS AND CASH	1210	1299
BANK ACCOUNT	1200	1209

Liabilities

CREDITORS : SHORT TERM	2100	2199	
TAXATION	2210	2299	
OTHER CREDITORS	2300	2399	
VAT LIABILITY	2200	2209	
GENERAL LIABILITY	9900	9999	(V5 only)

Financed By

SHARE CAPITAL	3000	3099
RESERVES	3100	3299

Creating or Altering Account Codes

This is carried out through the Nominal Ledger. Choose **Nominal Ledger** from the Main menu and then **Nominal Account Structure**. Then choose **Account Names**, you will then see the following data entry screen.

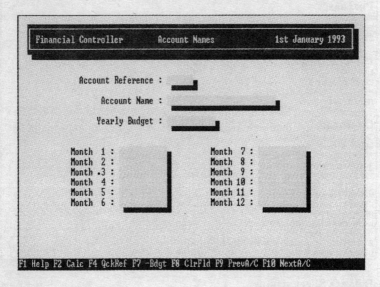

The data to be entered is:

Account Reference
From four to six digits (numbers) can be used, the existing ranges of codes and code groups are shown above. You need a good reason to choose account references outside of the ranges shown as you will have to reorganise the way your accounts are displayed (by altering the account groupings).

You will be asked if the code is a new one, if you enter an existing code, the rest of the details will be displayed.

Account Name
Up to 25 characters can be used to identify the code and if a name already exists, you can alter this to whatever you want.

Remember that **F8** will delete the original name.

Budget Values

If you are intending to use budgets within your organisation then you can enter a budget for the year, the monthly figures will be automatically calculated from this.

If you want to alter the budget for any month, retype the figure and the overall yearly figure will also be adjusted. You can then compare actual expenditure with the budgets throughout the year, this will give you more control over your expenditure.

When you have finished you can **ESC** and **POST** the details.

If you want to delete codes it is very simple; just enter the code and **ESC**. You will then be given (among others options) the chance to delete the code.

Account Groups

If you want to change the Account groups then you will need to select either the Profit and Loss or Balance Sheet Structure. Then choose **E** for Edit.

The options work in a similar way, as an illustration the options for the Profit and Loss Account are shown below.

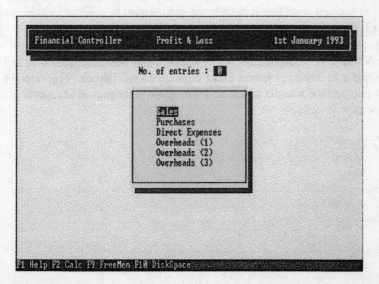

Following from this the actual groupings are displayed, to change either the names or the code groupings simply move the cursor, make the alteration and **return**.

The data entry screen is shown below.

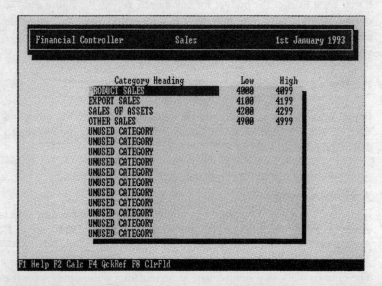

```
Financial Controller          Sales              1st January 1993


                    Category Heading          Low      High
             PRODUCT SALES                    4900     4099
             EXPORT SALES                     4100     4199
             SALES OF ASSETS                  4200     4299
             OTHER SALES                      4900     4999
             UNUSED CATEGORY
             UNUSED CATEGORY
             UNUSED CATEGORY
             UNUSED CATEGORY
             UNUSED CATEGORY
             UNUSED CATEGORY
             UNUSED CATEGORY
             UNUSED CATEGORY
             UNUSED CATEGORY
             UNUSED CATEGORY

F1 Help F2 Calc F4 QckRef F8 ClrFld
```

If the Balance Sheet does not balance, it is possible that you have used an account code that is outside the groups used to construct either the Trading, Profit and Loss Account or the Balance Sheet.

There is a further option within the Nominal Accounts Structure and this is to display or print a Chart of the Accounts Layout. This displays or prints the account groups and the layout of the printed accounts.

Entering the Opening Balances

> It is extremely important before entering any data that you decide how you are going to account for VAT. If you decide to work on a VAT cash accounting basis then you must make sure that you have set this up in the Company Preferences screen (Utilities and then Defaults).

Entering the Amounts Due to / from the Business

To enter the amounts due to / from the business (at the date you want the computerised accounts to begin) involves several stages:

* entering the figures into the program
* printing the Trial Balance resulting from those entries
* journalising out those balances (so that all that is left is a record of the amounts owed to and owed by your business)

Entering the Amount Due to Your Organisation

From the Main menu select **Sales Ledger** and then **Batched Data Entry** and finally **Sales Invoices** (and / or Sales Credit Notes).

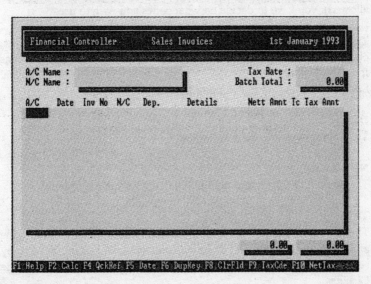

You should enter following data:

A/C
The account reference for the supplier (remember **F4** will bring up a list of the existing codes).

Date
The date the transaction took place (i.e. the invoice date), again the date has to be entered as a six digit number.

Inv No
The invoice number of the transaction, if this doesn't fit exactly then abbreviate it sensibly.

N/C
The Nominal Account Code for the transaction, for the opening balances all the items should be coded to the Suspense account code **9998**.

Dep
If you want to analyse your figures by department then you should enter the department code here (up to three digits, only numbers are allowed), you have to decide on what codes you wish to use.

To set up a departmental structure use the Utilities menu and then choose Departments. You can get reports on departmental costings from the Report Generator (DEPT report in the Sales Ledger, Nominal Ledger and Management Reports sections).

Details
Text which describes the transaction.

Nett Amnt
The amount of the invoice nett of VAT (before VAT is added).

Tc
The tax code (normally **T0** is zero rated, **T1** is the standard VAT code and **T9** is used for no VAT), the codes can be changed or added to by selecting from the Main menu the Utilities menu and VAT Code Changes.

Tax Amnt
The VAT on the transaction.

Please note that:

* the totals for the Nett and Tax Amnt columns appear on the bottom of the screen.
* whenever you key in a code the relevant name appears on the screen (usually in the top few rows).

Entering the Amounts Due from Your Organisation
From the Main menu select **Purchase Ledger** and then **Batched Data Entry** and finally **Purchase Invoices**. The screen is very similar to the Sales Ledger and so is the data to be entered.

Journalising the Balances
Now that these amounts have been entered you have to journalise out the balances that exist on the Trial Balance (the purpose of entering the opening balances is to ensure that there is a record of how much is owed to and by your organisation).

To do this we need to know what the balances are, select from the Main menu **Nominal Ledger** and then **Trial Balance**, you should print the figures.

When you have printed out the Trial Balance, you will see that the figures are laid out in columns (debit and credit), there will be balances for any or all of the following:

Debtors Control Account
Creditors Control Account
Suspense Account
VAT Account

Now **ESC** back to the Nominal Ledger menu, select **Journal Entries** and enter the amount shown in the Trial Balance in the **opposite way** to that shown in the Trial Balance, i.e. if the figure is shown as a debit in the Trial Balance then you enter it into the journal as a credit. Journal Entries are dealt with in the section dealing with the Nominal Ledger.

Entering the Opening Trial Balance

The next step is to enter the figures reflecting the assets and liabilities of the business at the date you computerise the accounts. This also involves journalising the figures. This is quite simple, firstly write down the balances from your previous system (or get your accountant to do it for you) making sure that the total debits equal the total credits and enter them into the journal (N.B. enter them normally, if it is a debit balance enter it as such).

It is worthwhile when you have done this to print out the Trial Balance and to check it against the original figures (just to ensure you are starting with the right figures).

THE SALES LEDGER

From the Main menu you can choose any of the activities available within the program. Each of these will be dealt with in sequence.

Select the Sales Ledger and the following screen will be displayed.

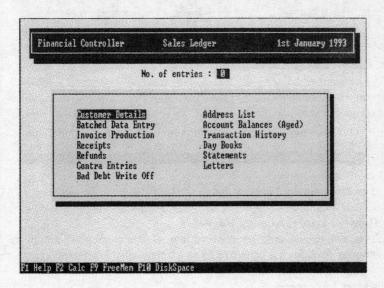

Customer Details

Where customers' or clients' details can be entered or altered, the use of this is detailed in the section dealing with setting up SAGE.

Address List

This lets you display the customer details you have entered into the system. You can accept the default answers to the questions or enter your own. You will be presented with this screen.

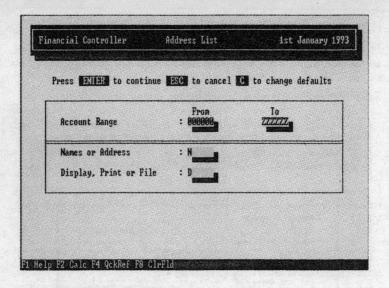

You can enter the following data:

(Lower / Upper) Account Range
You can decide only to print certain of the customers' details by entering specific data here (use **F4** to list the available references).

Names / Addresses
Answering **N** or **A** will produce a list of just the names or both the names and addresses.

Display, Printer or File
You can print out or display on screen or print to a file the names and addresses of your customers. The idea of printing to a file is so that the data can be edited in a word processing program or simply stored to be printed out later.

> If you choose Print to File (from any part of the program) the resulting file is called REPORT.001, REPORT.002, etc., and is stored in the SAGE directory.

You can use this option to print (sticky) address labels for mailing to customers.

Batched Data Entry

This is where sales invoices or sales credit notes are entered. It is called Batched Data Entry because the invoices are normally collected together into batches and posted together (although you can post as many or as few as you find convenient).

You have to post the entries once you have filled the data entry screen (i.e. after entering 12 transactions).

After selecting **Batched Data Entry** you have to choose either **Sales Invoices** or **Sales Credit Notes**. The data and screens are identical for each and the data to be entered was dealt with in the section on starting SAGE.

Account Balances (Aged)

Choosing this option produces a list of the amounts due to your firm in date order so that you can see who has owed you money for how long, which is vital for credit control purposes. You will need to answer certain questions to produce the listing (in a similar way to the Address List screen).

The Date of Report field allows you to date the report differently from the system date if you wish. You can scroll across the screen to see the breakdown by age of each debt by using the cursor keys.

Invoice Production

One of the interesting aspects of the way SAGE integrates the activities is the production of invoices. The advantage here is that when you produce (most types of) invoice the Stock and Sales Ledgers will be automatically updated. This is obviously time saving and avoids the possibility of error when entering data more than once into the system.

The first screen looks like this:

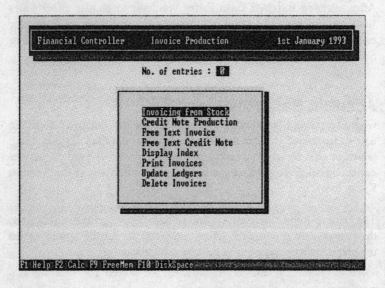

Invoicing from Stock

We will deal with each of these, firstly Invoicing from Stock. The screen is shown opposite.

The earlier versions of SAGE differ from the one shown here, there are three data entry screens which will appear one after the other.

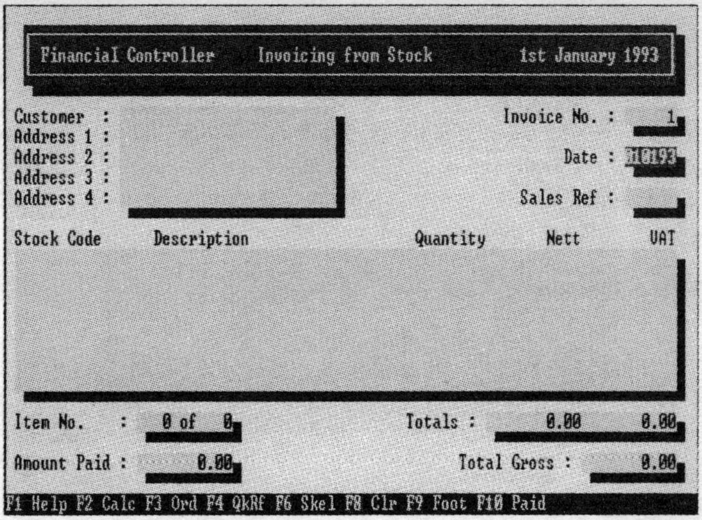

```
┌──────────────────────────────────────────────────────────────┐
│ ┌──────────────────────────────────────────────────────────┐ │
│ │ Financial Controller    Invoicing from Stock   1st January 1993 │ │
│ └──────────────────────────────────────────────────────────┘ │
│  Customer  :                              Invoice No. :     1  │
│  Address 1 :                                                   │
│  Address 2 :                                 Date : 010193     │
│  Address 3 :                                                   │
│  Address 4 :                               Sales Ref :         │
│                                                               │
│  Stock Code   Description          Quantity      Nett     VAT │
│                                                               │
│                                                               │
│                                                               │
│                                                               │
│                                                               │
│  Item No.   :   0 of  0            Totals :    0.00     0.00  │
│                                                               │
│  Amount Paid :    0.00            Total Gross :         0.00  │
│──────────────────────────────────────────────────────────────│
│ F1 Help F2 Calc F3 Ord F4 QkRf F6 Skel F8 Clr F9 Foot F10 Paid│
└──────────────────────────────────────────────────────────────┘
```

The first screen is where the customer details are entered, the Invoice
No. is incremented (added by one) for every invoice produced so that
the invoice numbers are created in sequence. You may alter the
invoice number if you want to.

Much of the remainder of the data is entered automatically by the
program (e.g. the customer details appear once you have entered the
Sales Ref(erence). It is possible to enter new customer details, if you
enter a code that does not exist then you will be asked if this is a new
customer. If you answer Y(es) then the screen for entering new
customer details will automatically appear.

The figures for the totals are for the invoice as a whole and are
therefore cumulative.

The next screen (which automatically will appear when you press F3),
displays details of the customer so that you can alter them if you wish.

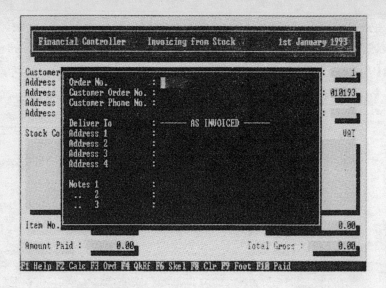

The next screen in this sequence is for the entering of stock details onto the invoice (this can be used to enter details of items that are not recorded in the stock records). It automatically appears when you move to the stock code field.

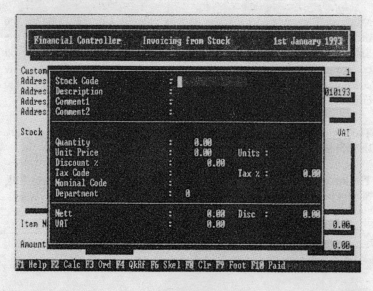

The Nominal Code is the code which you want posted with the details (normally a Sales code).

The nominal code MUST be entered otherwise the ledgers will not be posted.

The final screen of the sequence appears when you press **F9**, this is the footings screen and allows you to enter or alter the details.

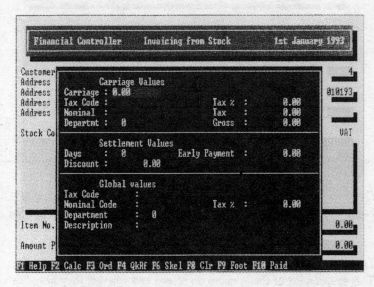

Credit Note Production
This is the opposite of Invoicing from Stock and both the details to be entered and the screens themselves are similar.

Free Text Invoice / Credit Note
It is only the second of the three screens that differs from the previous options. This option can be used where the invoice details do not fit into the previous format (e.g. where you want to enter some text) or where it is not a stock item.

Please note that Free Text Invoicing does not update the Stock records automatically although the ledgers are updated.

The screen below will appear when you enter the Description field and **return**:

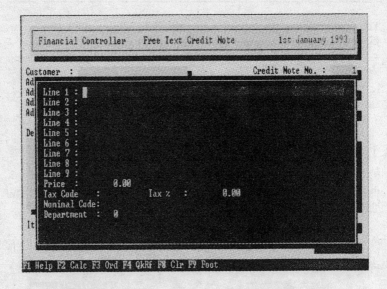

Display Index

This shows a list of the invoices on screen and whether they have been printed and/or posted to the ledger. You can look at the details of any item by moving the cursor over the item and **return**ing.

Print Invoices

You can request that certain or all invoices to be printed. If you want to print an invoice that has already been printed you need to answer **Y** to the prompt IGNORE PRINTED FLAG (the flag is set so that invoices are not normally printed again).

Update Ledgers

This must be carried out in order for the Ledgers to be posted with the details you have entered onto the invoices. A report should be printed out so that you have confirmation that the ledgers have actually been updated and if not why (so that you can take remedial action).

The most common causes for the ledgers not to be updated are not entering a Nominal code or not entering a Sales reference.

Delete Invoices

As the name suggests this allows you to delete chosen invoices. Please be careful if you use this option only to delete the invoices you want to (please note that it is possible to delete more than you want to if you do not take care to change the default settings).

Transaction History

You can display or print a listing of all the transactions that have taken place within an account or accounts by answering the questions that appear on the screen.

All unpaid invoices are marked by an asterisk (*) beside the value.
Partly paid invoices have a (p) beside the value.
Fully paid invoices are not marked.

Receipts

Here you would enter the money received from your credit customers (the customers who buy on credit and are entered into the Sales Ledger). The data entry screen is shown below:

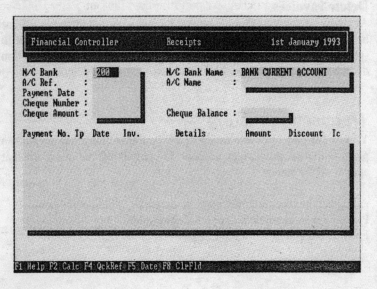

The entries you can make are:

N/C Bank
You can alter this if you have more than one bank account.

A/C Ref
The reference for the customer (use **F4** if you cannot remember it).

Payment Date
The date the money was received.

Cheque Number
Optional, you can enter the customer's cheque number, this may be useful if there is any problem in the future.

Cheque Amount
How much the cheque is for.

After entering this data the screen will display the outstanding invoices waiting to be paid off.

You will then be asked whether the method of payment is **Automatic** or **Manual**. If you choose Automatic then the outstanding invoices are cleared in sequence starting at the top. If you choose Manual you can select which invoices are to be cleared (partly or wholly) by moving the cursor down and then **return**. If you make a mistake simply move the cursor over the transaction again and **return**, this will clear it.

Finally you will be asked if you want to **POST**, **EDIT** or **ABANDON**, this allows you to alter errors before you post incorrect data.

Payments On Account
If you cannot match the receipt with the invoice then you can treat the money as a payment on account.

When you want to match the payment on account with a particular invoice, choose **Receipts** and then enter the details but put **zero** as the cheque amount.

Then choose **Manual** and move the cursor to the payment on account and **return**, then choose which type of payment it is (full or part) and then move the cursor to the invoice you are setting it against and **return**. The amount will be deducted from the invoice.

Day Books

After choosing this option you will be presented with four choices:

Sales Invoices
Sales Credit Notes
Sales Receipts
Sales Discounts

The Day Books list all the sales transactions in order and for each you will be asked to decide on several parameters.

Nominal Account Range and **(Lower / Upper) Transaction Number**

You can decide to list only a certain range of transactions, or you can list all of them (if you want to look up the transaction numbers use the Audit Trail to list them).

Date Range from / to

You can decide between which dates you want the data for.

Display, Printer or File

As with the other listings you can display on screen, print to paper or save the data in a file.

Tax Code

You can list out data for all the codes or for selected ones.

Refunds

This is the option that lets you account for situations where your sale has been returned or cancelled by the client. There are two possibilities:

Cancel Cheque
Refund Invoice

Cancel Cheque

This is used in situations where you want to cancel an existing receipt from a customer (or Purchase Ledger payment). The screen is shown opposite.

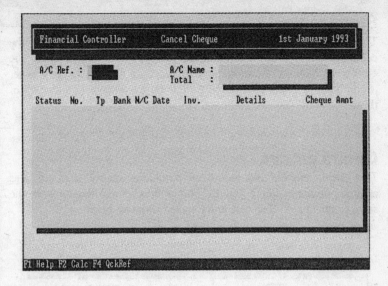

The data to be entered is:

A/C Ref
The reference of the customer (use **F4** if you have forgotten it). At this point all the money that has been received is shown on the screen. Move the cursor over the invoice to be dealt with and **return**.

If you make a mistake and choose the wrong invoice then simply select it again and **return**.

Finally **ESC** and decide whether to **POST**, **EDIT** or **ABANDON**.

If you get an error message saying use the
BOUNCED CHEQUE OPTION
you can use this option to deal with it.

Refund Invoice
The screen is very similar to the Cancel Cheque option, please note that this screen only displays fully paid invoices and it can be used to refund sales (or purchase) invoices.

You may not wish to use this option if you are using VAT cash accounting as the VAT is not accounted for.

Statements

These are summaries of the amounts due to your firm from the customer and can be printed out so that you can send them to the customer. You will be asked several questions which you can answer if you want to select specific customers or just **return** to select all of them.

Contra entries

This option enables you to set off purchases against sales or sales against purchases where you are both selling to and buying from the same organisation. The data entry screen is shown below:

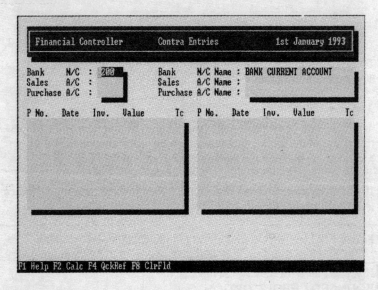

Sales A/C / Purchase A/C (references)
The account references relating to the transaction. After these have been entered the screen will display all the outstanding invoices for each.

To select an invoice to contra, move the cursor over it and press **return** (to cancel a contra repeat the process). When finished **ESC** and **POST** if correct. Please note that the totals for each ledger must agree before you can post them. You will not be allowed to post the items unless the contra entry is valid.

Letters

You can automatically print letters to your customers containing certain pre-defined data, the data entry screen is shown below:

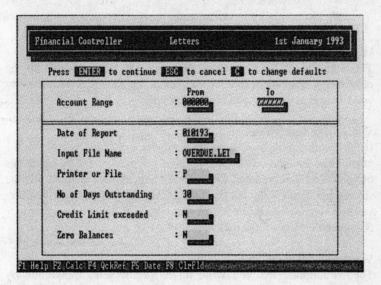

You will be asked to either accept the default answers to the questions or to substitute alternative criteria. The Input File Name is the file containing the draft letter and you should accept the default unless you have created a customised letter of your own.

> Previous versions of SAGE consist of two screens (rather than the one shown here).

Bad Debts Write Off

Sometimes you will not be able to recover an amount due to you and will have to write it off.

After selecting this you will be presented with three options:

Write Off Account

This asks for the Sales Account Reference and will write off **all** the outstanding amounts in this account (there is a further screen allowing you to see exactly what you are writing off).

Write Off Small Values

If the amounts outstanding are small (under £100) and not worth the hassle then you can write those specific transactions off by using this option. You will be asked for the maximum amount to write off, the screen will then display all the outstanding items below this amount, you will then be asked to confirm each write-off (type **Y** to confirm or **N** to take the item off the list).

Write Off Transactions

The third option lets you write off a specific sales transaction by entering the Transaction Number to Write Off (use the Audit Trail or the Transaction History option to identify the transaction if you are unsure of its number).

VAT is not adjusted for when you use this option, so if you have a bad debt for which you can reclaim the VAT which you have already accounted for, you should not use this option.

The Purchase Ledger

The screen shows the various options within this ledger.

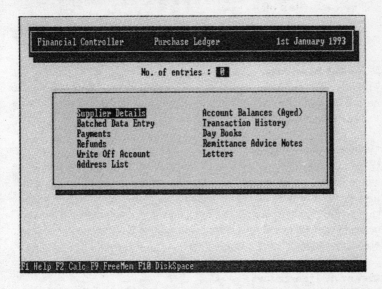

As you can see the options are similar to those available within the Sales Ledger, this is logical since the two ledgers are mirror images of each other. To avoid too much repetition only where the Purchase Ledger options differ from the Sales Ledger will there be any notes, otherwise you can refer to the relevant section within the Sales Ledger.

The following differences are worth noting:

Write Off Accounts
This is the only write off option available in the Purchase Ledger.

Remittance Advice Notes
These can be printed out to accompany the payments you make to your suppliers to identify what the payment are for.

Letters
This option lets you send letters to your suppliers using a standard layout. Please note that the default letter (OVERDUE.LET) is only really suitable for mailing customers who owe you money and you may want to create your own.

THE NOMINAL LEDGER

This ledger enables you to produce the accounts and various useful reports, the options are shown below.

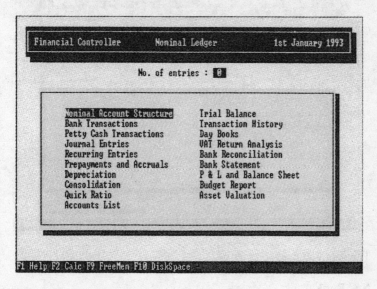

```
┌─────────────────────────────────────────────────────────────┐
│ Financial Controller        Nominal Ledger        1st January 1993 │
│                                                               │
│                    No. of entries : 0                         │
│  ┌─────────────────────────────────────────────────────────┐ │
│  │ Nominal Account Structure    Trial Balance              │ │
│  │ Bank Transactions            Transaction History        │ │
│  │ Petty Cash Transactions      Day Books                  │ │
│  │ Journal Entries              VAT Return Analysis        │ │
│  │ Recurring Entries            Bank Reconciliation        │ │
│  │ Prepayments and Accruals     Bank Statement             │ │
│  │ Depreciation                 P & L and Balance Sheet    │ │
│  │ Consolidation                Budget Report              │ │
│  │ Quick Ratio                  Asset Valuation            │ │
│  │ Accounts List                                           │ │
│  └─────────────────────────────────────────────────────────┘ │
│                                                               │
│ F1 Help F2 Calc F9 FreeMem F10 DiskSpace                      │
└─────────────────────────────────────────────────────────────┘
```

Each of the options will be dealt with in sequence.

Nominal Account Structure

This was dealt with in the section on setting up SAGE.

Bank Transactions

There are two options here:

Bank Payments
Bank Receipts

The data entry screens are identical and look like this:

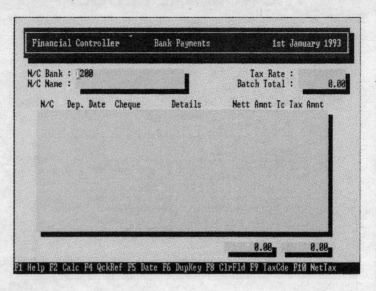

```
┌─────────────────────────────────────────────────────────────────┐
│  Financial Controller      Bank Payments        1st January 1993 │
│                                                                   │
│  N/C Bank : 200                          Tax Rate :               │
│  N/C Name :                              Batch Total :      0.00   │
│                                                                   │
│    N/C   Dep. Date  Cheque       Details      Nett Amnt Tc Tax Amnt│
│                                                                   │
│                                                                   │
│                                                                   │
│                                                                   │
│                                                                   │
│                                                                   │
│                                                                   │
│                                              0.00       0.00      │
│ F1 Help F2 Calc F4 QckRef F5 Date F6 DupKey F8 ClrFld F9 TaxCde F10 NetTax│
└─────────────────────────────────────────────────────────────────┘
```

The data you need to enter is:

N/C Bank
If you have set up more than one business bank account you may need to change this.

N/C
The nominal code for the payment (or receipt).

Dep
If you have created a departmental structure then you can enter the department code here.

Date
The date of the transaction.

Cheque
The cheque number, this can be extremely useful when you want to reconcile the Bank account or otherwise check your payments (or receipts).

Details
Text to identify the transaction.

Nett Amnt
The amount of the cheque **before** VAT (i.e. Nett).

Tc
The tax code for the transaction (normally **T0** for zero rate, **T1** for standard rate or **T9** for no VAT).

Tax Amnt
The amount of VAT (this is calculated automatically by the program).

Petty Cash Transactions
These can be either:

Cash Payments
Cash Receipts

The data to be entered is very similar to the Bank Payments screen.

To transfer money from the bank account to the petty cash or vice versa you need to use the journal.

Journal Entries

Used to transfer amounts from one ledger account code to another.

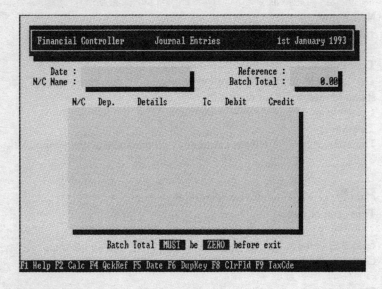

```
Financial Controller        Journal Entries        1st January 1993

    Date :                              Reference :
N/C Name :                              Batch Total :        0.00

          N/C    Dep.    Details     Tc    Debit     Credit




                 Batch Total  MUST  be  ZERO  before exit
F1 Help F2 Calc F4 QckRef F5 Date F6 DupKey F8 ClrFld F9 TaxCde
```

The journal must total to zero before you can post it (this means that the total debits equal the total credit entries). If you are ever in the unfortunate situation where they do not (and you cannot see why) then post the balance to the Suspense account. You can make the necessary adjustment later on.

The data to be entered within this screen is:

Date
The date you wish to assign to the journal entry (**F5** to enter the current date).

Reference
Any reference you want to identify the journal entry.

N/C
The nominal codes for the debit and credit entries (remember **F4** will bring up a list of the codes).

Dep
A department analysis code (if you are using one).

Details

Text to identify the purpose of the journal (it is best to enter a meaningful phrase as you can then understand what you have done at a later stage).

Tc

The tax code.

Debit / Credit

Enter the amount in the relevant column

Finally **ESC** and **POST** the completed journal (or **ABANDON** or edit it).

Recurring Entries

This menu option lets you set up regular transactions so that you do not have to keep entering them. This is useful for standing orders or any other payments made on a regular basis.

The data entry screen is shown opposite, there are a few differences between this screen and ones already encountered.

Tp (transaction type)

You have to enter one of the following into this field:

BP   (bank payment)

JD   (journal debit)

JC   (journal credit)

Date

The date you want the transaction to be posted to the ledgers. **F5** will print the word TODAY as a date. This will ensure that items are posted on the date the Month End routines are carried out.

Ref

You can enter any (up to) six digit alphanumeric into this field.

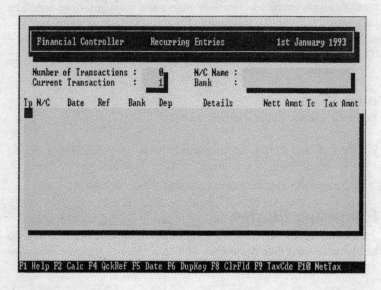

If you have already set up some recurring entries then when you select this option they will be displayed automatically. To delete one that exists simply enter **D** in the **Tp** field.

The data is posted when you carry out the Month End routines (from the Utilities menu).

Prepayments and Accruals

Whenever you pay a supplier or receive some types of income, the amount is for a period of time which may go over the end of your accounting period (be it monthly or yearly).

The amount that is for the time **beyond** your end of period accounting date is called a prepayment (where you have paid the amount) or an accrual (where a customer has paid you or you have received goods or services which the supplier has not invoiced to you by the end of the accounting period).

You have the option of choosing either Prepayments or Accruals, the screens and data entry are very similar.

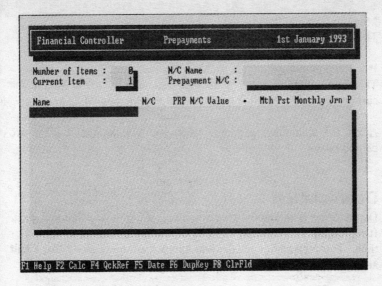

Number of Items :   8   N/C Name   :
Current Item   :   1   Prepayment N/C :

Name   N/C   PRP N/C Value   •   Mth Pst Monthly Jrn P

F1 Help F2 Calc F4 QckRef F5 Date F6 DupKey F8 ClrFld

The data to be entered in this option is:

Name
Up to 25 characters to describe the transaction, however it is best to
use only 19 as only this number will appear in the Audit trail.

N/C
The nominal code for the transaction.

PRP N/C / ACR N/C
This will show either of the above depending upon whether you are
using the prepayment or accrual option. They stand for Prepayment
Nominal Code (or Accrual Nominal Code).

Value
The amount of the prepayment or accrual.

Mth
The number of months the payment is to be spread over.

Pst
This shows the number of months that have already been posted for
that prepayment or accrual.

Monthly Jrn
The actual value that will be posted the next month.

P
This field will show a star if the item has already been posted in the current month.

Again the amounts are posted when the Month End routines are carried out.

Depreciation

Depreciation is an amount that is written off the value of a fixed asset. It represents the reduction in value of that asset through wear and or time. The depreciation for the year appears as an expense in the Profit and Loss Account and reduces the overall profit.

There are three methods of calculating depreciation within SAGE:

Straight Line
This is where the (same) percentage is deducted from the value, a straight line of 10% would write off the total value of the asset in ten years, thus the amount charged to the depreciation account is the same every year.

An asset costs £200 and the percentage depreciation is 20%

Year	Asset Value	Depreciation
one	200	40
two	160	40
three	120	40
four	80	40

Reducing Balance
The same percentage is charged per year but the balance left at the end of the year is reduced by the depreciation charge and the next year's depreciation is worked on the reduced balance.

An asset costs £200 and the percentage depreciation is 20%

Year	Asset Value	Depreciation
one	200	40
two	160	32
three	128	26
four	102	20

You can see from the illustrations that the straight line method writes off the asset totally over a period of years whereas the reducing balance method will leave a small balance which will never actually become zero.

Write Off

This writes off the remaining balance of the item totally. It can be used either to write off small amounts remaining in the asset account or to write off an asset that suddenly becomes worthless.

The screen will display the depreciating assets you have already set up. When altering items or entering new items to charge depreciation on, the data to be entered is:

Name

Up to 25 characters (but only the first 19 will be shown in the Audit trail).

N/C

The nominal code for the depreciation account for the item (remember F4 will bring up a list of the Nominal codes).

Value

The present value of the item you want to depreciate.

Tp

The type of depreciation i.e.

S	straight line
R	reducing balance
W	write off
D	delete the item from the list

%

The percentage figure for the depreciation.

Amount

This is calculated for you and shows the amount to be written off the value of the asset per month.

Current

The current value of the item after deducting the depreciation charged to date.

P

A star will be displayed if the depreciation has been charged for the current month.

Consolidation

This consolidates or joins together the figures for the subsidiary companies into the main or holding company. It can only be used if you have an organisation that consists of a holding company and one or more subsidiary companies.

It is necessary to have selected the Parent company before proceeding with this option and the Parent company should not have any data. You must clear the Parent company files of data by using the Rebuild option within Utilities (Data File Changes) and to answer No to the question about existing data.

Quick Ratio

This is a reporting mechanism to let you see the current liquid (cash flow) position of the business, it can be used to display the bank and cash positions together with any other items you are interested in (e.g. how much you are owed or owe at that point in time). Once you have set up the account codes you want displayed then you simply choose to view the option and the latest position will be displayed on screen.

Accounts List

This was also dealt with in the section on setting up SAGE.

Trial Balance

This was looked at when starting SAGE and is a display of the balances on each and every ledger account. From the Trial Balance the Profit and Loss Account and the Balance Sheet are calculated.

Transaction History

As with the Sales and Purchase Ledgers you can display the history of any or all of the Nominal Ledger accounts (the history simply means the transactions that have taken place within that account code).

You are able to choose the upper and lower codes and whether you want the report displayed on screen or printed in a similar way to other reports.

Daybooks

Manual accounting systems of any size keep daybooks which are records of the day to day transactions of the business, SAGE has an option to allow you to display or print out the data so that you can look at it. The daybooks are:

Bank Payments
Bank Receipts
Cash Payments
Cash Receipts
Journal Entries

You will be asked for the upper and lower transaction numbers and the date ranges you are interested in looking at, the idea being that you can define the data you want to look at very precisely.

VAT Return Analysis (v5 only)

This option accumulates all the VAT amounts by VAT code and type of transactions and displays the total inputs and outputs for each.

After choosing this option you will be asked for certain criteria most of which are self-explanatory:

Tax Code
If you use the default tax codes simply **return** over this question.

Tax by Invoice or Payment (only for VAT cash accounting)
If you want VAT to be assessed when you receive the money from customers or actually pay it to your suppliers then type **P**.

Include Reconciled Items
If you answer **N**(o) to this then items already included in previous VAT reconciliations will not be included again.

Set Reconciliation Flags
If you answer **Y**(es) to this then items included in this VAT reconciliation will not be included again on subsequent reconciliations.

After accepting or altering the default settings, the screen will then display a summary of your VAT return and if you **return** on any item, you will be able to see details of how the figure is made up.

After doing this it is necessary to journalise the VAT balance by moving the balancing figure from the Tax Control Account (2200) to the Tax Liability Account (2201), this will make your accounts correct and will show the amount due to the Customs and Excise in the Tax Liability Account. It will also clear the Tax Control Account so that it can be used for the next month's figures. When the VAT due is paid to the C&E, it should be coded to the Tax Liability account.

Bank Reconciliation
This option lets you compare your bank account records in SAGE with your actual bank statements. The first step is to move the cursor onto all the items that agree and **return** on each (this will highlight it in a different colour). The remaining items that do not correspond are then dealt with.

Items appear on the bank statement but not in your accounting records can be entered into SAGE by pressing **F9** and then entering the item by entering the details.

Items appearing in the reconciliation statement that are included in your accounting records but do not appear on the bank statement need to be checked since they are either incorrect entries or have not gone through the bank.

Bank Statement

This lets you print or view a report of the transactions on your bank account(s) for specific ranges. The screen showing the options is below.

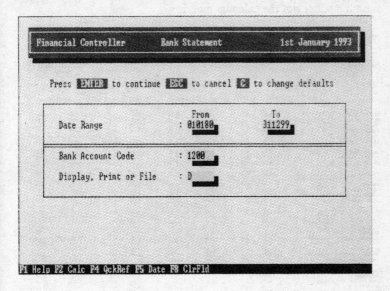

```
Financial Controller        Bank Statement        1st January 1993


    Press ENTER to continue ESC to cancel C to change defaults

    ┌─────────────────────────────────────────────────────────────┐
    │                              From             To             │
    │   Date Range            : 010180         311299              │
    ├─────────────────────────────────────────────────────────────┤
    │   Bank Account Code     : 1200                               │
    │   Display, Print or File  : D                               │
    └─────────────────────────────────────────────────────────────┘




 F1 Help F2 Calc P4 QckRef F5 Date F8 ClrFld
```

P&L and Balance Sheet

This will produce a set of accounts for the month and will also show the accumulated figures for the year. The monthly figures represent the actual changes or transactions that have taken place within the last month, it is possible therefore to have negative figures within the Balance Sheet for example where the Debtors figure has reduced.

It is important at this stage to save the month's figures onto a floppy disc so that the files can be recreated either because of a problem in the next month or to look at again. To do this simply Backup the files by using the Utilities menu.

> Keep all backups safe by writing a description of the contents on the label and write-protect the disc so that it cannot be accidentally erased. Then put the disc somewhere safe.
>
> It would be sensible to make two copies of the backups (just in case).

Budget Report

If you have set up budgets then you can use this report to print out or view the differences between the actual figures for the month and the budgeted figures. You will be asked for the Month, this is the financial month number **not** the calendar month.

The report will look similar to this:

		MONTHLY				YEAR-TO-DATE		
	Actual	Ratio(%)	Budget	Variance	Actual	Ratio(%)	Budget	Variance
PRODUCT SALES	0.00	0.0	0.00	0.00	0.00	0.0	0.00	0.00
EXPORT SALES	0.00	0.0	0.00	0.00	0.00	0.0	0.00	0.00
SALES OF ASSETS	0.00	0.0	0.00	0.00	0.00	0.0	0.00	0.00
OTHER SALES	0.00	0.0	0.00	0.00	0.00	0.0	0.00	0.00
Sales	0.00	0.0	0.00	0.00	0.00	0.0	0.00	0.00
PURCHASES	0.00	0.0	0.00	0.00	0.00	0.0	0.00	0.00
PURCHASE CHARGES	0.00	0.0	0.00	0.00	0.00	0.0	0.00	0.00
STOCK	0.00	0.0	0.00	0.00	0.00	0.0	0.00	0.00
Purchases	0.00	0.0	0.00	0.00	0.00	0.0	0.00	0.00
LABOUR	0.00	0.0	0.00	0.00	0.00	0.0	0.00	0.00
COMMISSIONS	0.00	0.0	0.00	0.00	0.00	0.0	0.00	0.00
MISCELLANEOUS EXPENSES	0.00	0.0	0.00	0.00	0.00	0.0	0.00	0.00
SALES PROMOTION	0.00	0.0	0.00	0.00	0.00	0.0	0.00	0.00
	0.00	0.0	0.00	0.00	0.00	0.0	0.00	0.00
Gross Profit	0.00	0.0	0.00	0.00	0.00	0.0	0.00	0.00
SALARIES AND WAGES	0.00	0.0	0.00	0.00	0.00	0.0	0.00	0.00
RENT AND RATES	0.00	0.0	0.00	0.00	0.00	0.0	0.00	0.00
HEAT, LIGHT AND POWER	0.00	0.0	0.00	0.00	0.00	0.0	0.00	0.00
MOTOR EXPENSES	0.00	0.0	0.00	0.00	0.00	0.0	0.00	0.00
TRAVELLING AND ENTERTAINMENT	0.00	0.0	0.00	0.00	0.00	0.0	0.00	0.00
PRINTING AND STATIONERY	0.00	0.0	0.00	0.00	0.00	0.0	0.00	0.00
PROFESSIONAL FEES	0.00	0.0	0.00	0.00	0.00	0.0	0.00	0.00
EQUIPMENT HIRE AND RENTAL	0.00	0.0	0.00	0.00	0.00	0.0	0.00	0.00
MAINTENANCE	0.00	0.0	0.00	0.00	0.00	0.0	0.00	0.00
BANK CHARGES AND INTEREST	0.00	0.0	0.00	0.00	0.00	0.0	0.00	0.00
DEPRECIATION	0.00	0.0	0.00	0.00	0.00	0.0	0.00	0.00
BAD DEBTS	0.00	0.0	0.00	0.00	0.00	0.0	0.00	0.00
GENERAL EXPENSES	0.00	0.0	0.00	0.00	0.00	0.0	0.00	0.00
	0.00	0.0	0.00	0.00	0.00	0.0	0.00	0.00
Nett Profit	0.00	0.0	0.00	0.00	0.00	0.0	0.00	0.00

You can use this report to give you more control over your expenditure by comparing actual with budgeted.

Asset Valuation

This report contains details of all the assets which you are depreciating with the values and type of depreciation shown. The **P** column shows whether the depreciation has been charged for the current month.

Nominal Ledger Items Appearing in v4 and Below

Monthly Accounts
This allows you to Create Month End Files and is dealt with in the Utilities section of this book.

Control Account History
These accounts record the posting of items to the Nominal Ledger, when (e.g.) a sales item is posted to the Nominal Ledger the rules of double entry are followed and a control account is created so that the rules of double entry are maintained. The options are:

Debtor's Control
Creditor's Control
Bank Account
Petty Cash
Tax Control

The Control Accounts keep a record of all items posted and you can print out a history of the transactions for each account.

PAYROLL

Rules and Regulations

In this chapter we will look at the rules and regulations about Tax and National Insurance.

The legal responsibility is on you to keep up to date with the legislation and to understand how to make the calculations, so you may have to obtain assistance from the Inland Revenue or from your accountant to make sure that you are both up to date and are interpreting the rules correctly. The Inland Revenue have many pamphlets and books which explain the law and these are normally free (as is the advice they will give you).

Please note that the rules can alter considerably from year to year and even within a tax year, so you must make sure that you receive and read the information sent to you by the Inland Revenue.

As far as the Inland Revenue are concerned, you must by law make deductions from your employees' pay for PAYE, NIC, SSP and SMP. We will look at each of these in turn.

PAYE

This means Pay As You Earn and is a method of collecting the tax from employees by making the employer deduct it before the employee gets his weekly or monthly pay. It is a very efficient method of collecting taxes from the government's point of view.

By law you have to work out the tax for each employee every time you pay them and to keep a record of these payments. Each month you have to pay the Inland Revenue the amount of tax you have deducted (if you are a very small business then it may be possible to pay over the tax and NIC (National Insurance Contributions) quarterly rather than monthly). At the end of the tax year you have to send them a summary of the year's figures.

It is important to realise that employees include anyone employed by your business to do work and includes directors and casual workers. There may be certain people who do work for you who are self-employed and special rules apply to these (which you can obtain from your local tax office). Obviously when you hire another firm or business (e.g. an accountant) then they will send you an invoice and you should not deduct tax from this.

If you are not sure of the status of anyone whom you pay money to, then you must check with the Inland Revenue as if you make a mistake and do not deduct tax then you may still be liable for the money.

Almost any payment to an employee is taxable, for example bonuses, tips and payments for private medicine plans. Again if you do not deduct tax when you should have, then you may be liable.

To help you calculate the tax, the Inland Revenue supply you with tax codes for each employee and tax tables (if you intend to manually calculate the tax). The tax year runs from 6th April to the 5th April of the following year.

PAYE Codes

Each employee is given a tax code from which the PAYE is calculated, the code consists of a combination of letters and numbers. Examples of these are shown below:

NT	No tax to be deducted
BR	Tax to be deducted at the basic rate, no allowances to be set against the tax.
Emergency code	A special code used, for example, where there is no P45 from the previous employment.
245H D0 F321	Examples of normal codes where allowances (such as personal allowances) have been set against taxable pay.

National Insurance

There are two types of National Insurance, Employee's and Employer's. You must deduct the employees' N.I. from their pay and account for this and the employer's N.I. at the same time as for the PAYE tax. The rules are similar to those outlined above.

Like PAYE tax there are lower limits below which an employee does not have to pay National Insurance contributions and in the case of N.I. there are upper limits, so that there is an effective maximum amount of money that an employee has to pay in N.I. contributions. There are also age limits and those below 16 and above pensionable age do not pay NICs (National Insurance Contributions).

N.I. contributions go towards providing retirement pensions and towards funding the National Health Service. An employee may be contracted into the government pension scheme (called **not contracted out**) or **contracted out**. If an employee is contracted out of the government scheme then they have to make payments to a private pension scheme (and these payments will normally be deducted from their pay).

As well as the employees' N.I. contribution, the employer has to pay their contribution towards the State Benefits, this is the employer's NIC and is **not** deducted from the employees' pay but is paid by the employer.

Statutory Sick Pay

Employers are legally obliged to provide sick pay for their employees. At present this is paid after the first four consecutive days of absence. It is paid as if it were normal pay and you as the employer can claim back a large (at present 80%) part of both the tax and N.I.C. paid under this scheme from the government.

There are several terms used with this scheme which need explanation (please note that these represent the current situation and are liable to change):

Period of incapacity for work (PIW)
Any period in excess of four days qualifies for SSP.

Linking
If there are two or more periods of PIW separated by less than eight weeks then they are treated as one period of PIW for calculation purposes.

Qualifying days
This means the days for which the employee is eligible to be paid SSP (normally those days the person would be at work if well).

Waiting days
The first three days of a PIW where the employee is not eligible for SSP (and for which you would pay them their normal pay).

There are certain situations where you do not pay SSP, for example, if the employee's earnings are below the lower NIC level, or if they are over pensionable age and so on (as with everything if you are unsure contact the DHSS or I.R.).

Also remember that SSP is paid in the same way as ordinary pay and the employee has to pay both tax and national insurance contributions.

Statutory Maternity Pay (SMP)
Like SSP this is paid for a limited period while an employee is off work. However this is slightly different as the employee has to be female and pregnant to qualify for this benefit.

It operates in a similar way to SSP and again there are special terms used:

EWC
This is the expected week of confinement (the week the baby is due).

QW
The qualifying week, the fifteenth week before the EWC.

MPP
The maternity pay period, this is the period of up to eighteen weeks for which you may have to pay SMP. The lady concerned can decide to some extent for which eighteen week period she will receive the SMP.

You should be supplied with a maternity certificate to provide medical evidence that a baby is due and when it is due (approximately).

Tax and National Insurance contributions still have to be deducted from the SMP payments.

Starting Off

When you start to use SAGE payroll, the initial payroll screen looks like this:

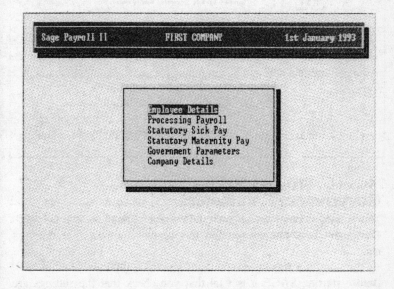

From this screen menu you can select all the other options within the program.

Remember that you must press the **return** key after entering new data.

Within the payroll option you can use the following keys to help you move around the screens and to bring up useful data, though not all keys work within each menu option.

↑ ↓	
→ ←	to move around a screen or onto the next
home end	to move to the start or end of a screen
pg up pg dn	to move onto the next screen of a series
F 1	the HELP key
F 2	the calculator (press ESC to exit)
F 3	the pop up key (provides useful data)
F 4	pops up the employee list (use it to move to another employee's record)
F 7	the quick reference key
F 8	clears the current field of its data
F 10 F 9	to move to the next employee / previous employee
CTRL →	moves along a field to let you edit the data

Government Parameters

The program comes set up with the current settings for the tax year. Obviously these can change and this option lets you alter them as necessary.

Before starting SAGE it is vital that you check that the settings are correct for the tax year you are dealing with.

To do this select Government Parameters from the original menu and the following screen will appear.

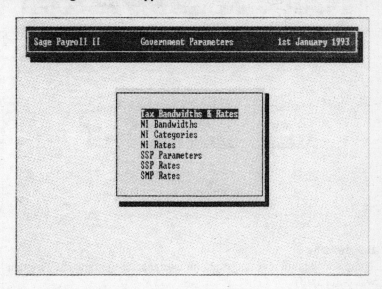

We will look at each of these in turn beginning with the first, Tax Bandwidths and Rates.

Tax Bandwidths and Rates

Select this and the screen (shown overleaf) will appear. You may need to change the figures in the Bandwidth column (the other figures will then automatically change).

To alter the figures in a bandwidth, **return** through the fields, or use the cursor keys, until you get to the required field. Then type in the new data and **return** to finish.

To create a new Bandwidth, type a new figure in the No. of Bandwidths field (note that there is one more Bandwidth than the number specified in this field, this is for the excess over the top rate).

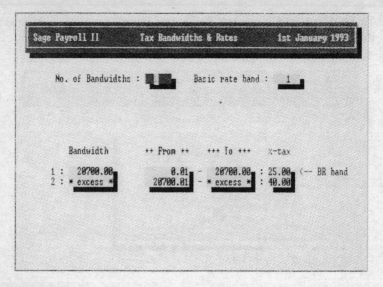

No. of Bandwidths : ▆▆   Basic rate band :   1

```
     Bandwidth       ++ From ++    +++ To +++    %-tax
1 :   20700.00          0.01  -    20700.00  : 25.00  <-- BR band
2 : * excess *       20700.01  -  * excess * : 40.00
```

Bandwidths

These are the different tax bands (in existence at the time the program was purchased).

From / To

The amounts of money in each tax band.

% - tax

The percentage of tax to be deducted from the amounts earned in each band.

BR band

Basic rate of taxable pay (normally this is Band 1).

ESC back to the previous menu when you have finished.

N.I. Bandwidths

Similar to the previous menu, this time you can alter the National Insurance limits in similar ways to the tax bandwidths.

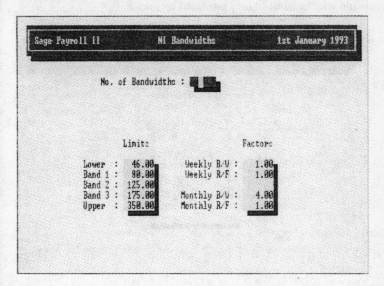

Limits
The limits are the figures for each band of N.I. deductions.

Factors
This column contains four fields each of which may need some explanation.

Weekly B/W and Monthly B/W
These show the steps that the income is to be assessed. The DHSS assesses weekly income in steps of one pound.

Weekly R/F and Monthly R/F
This is the 'table base rounding factor' and is used within the calculations of N.I. contributions for monthly paid employees'.

ESC back to the previous menu when you have finished.

N.I. Categories

Within this screen you can enter the categories of N.I. contributions and whether they are contracted in or contracted out of SERPS. You should use the latest figures produced by the I.R.

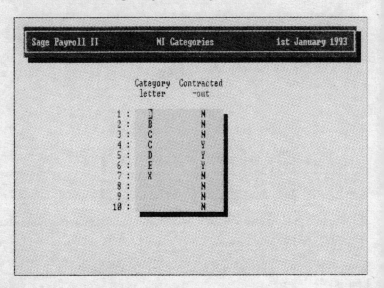

```
Sage Payroll II          NI Categories          1st January 1993


                  Category   Contracted
                   letter      -out

              1 :    J            N
              2 :    B            N
              3 :    C            N
              4 :    C            Y
              5 :    D            Y
              6 :    E            Y
              7 :    X            N
              8 :                 N
              9 :                 N
             10 :                 N
```

ESC back to the previous menu when you have finished.

N.I. Rates

The left hand side of the screen shows the N.I. bandwidths defined earlier and the various percentages payable by the employer and employee. You will need to alter these if the rates change.

The Categories are displayed in sequence (use **Pg Up** and **Pg Dn** to move between them).

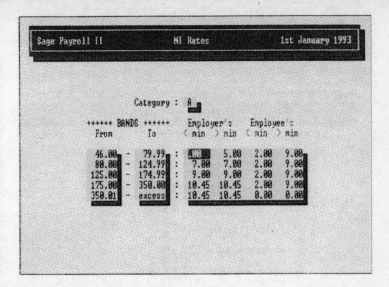

```
                    Category : A

++++++ BANDS ++++++      Employer's      Employee's
  From          To       < min  > min    < min  > min

  46.00   -   79.99  :    6.00   5.00     2.00   9.00
  80.00   -  124.99  :    7.00   7.00     2.00   9.00
 125.00   -  174.99  :    9.00   9.00     2.00   9.00
 175.00   -  350.00  :   10.45  10.45     2.00   9.00
 350.01   -  excess  :   10.45  10.45     0.00   0.00
```

Please note that the figures in the right hand columns are percentages
not actual figures.

ESC back to the previous menu when you have finished.

SSP Parameters

This screen shows the current settings, they should be altered if the rates change:

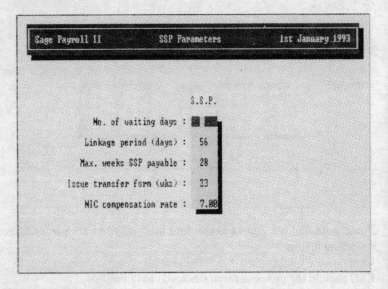

```
Sage Payroll II          SSP Parameters          1st January 1993



                                    S.S.P.

                 No. of waiting days :  █ █

              Linkage period (days) :   56

            Max. weeks SSP payable :   28

           Issue transfer form (wks) :   23

           NIC compensation rate :    7.00
```

No. of waiting days
How many days does an employee have to wait before qualifying for Statutory Sick Pay.

Linkage period (days)
The period used to link two periods of SSP qualification together, if a person falls ill within this period their absence is linked to the previous period of SSP.

Max. weeks SSP payable
The maximum period of payment of SSP.

Issue transfer form (wks)
The week within the maximum period of SSP payment that an employee must be notified that time on the scheme is running out and that they will need to transfer to the State scheme.

NIC compensation rate
This is fixed by the DHSS and will only need changing if the rate alters.

ESC back to the previous menu when you have finished.

SSP Rates

This screen shows the current settings for Statutory Sick Pay and they can be changed if necessary.

When you alter the figures in the Threshold columns, the figures in the From and To columns also change to correspond. You can also alter the rate figure.

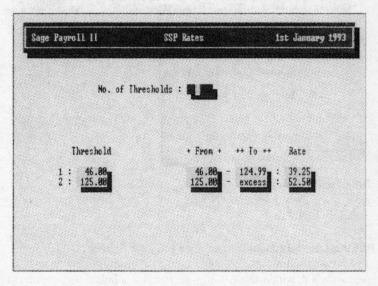

ESC back to the previous menu when you have finished.

SMP Rates

This shows the figures for Statutory Maternity Pay. The screen shows the higher and lower rates and the maximum weeks that can be paid at the higher and lower rates. All the figures in this screen can be altered.

The NIC compensation rate is a percentage fixed by the DHSS (as with the SSP parameters).

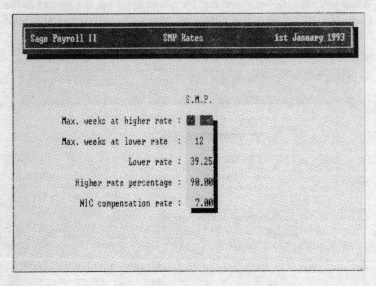

ESC back to the previous menu when you have finished.

Company Details

Company Details

One of the first tasks you will have to do before SAGE Payroll can function properly is to enter information about the firm.

The menu for Company Details looks like this:

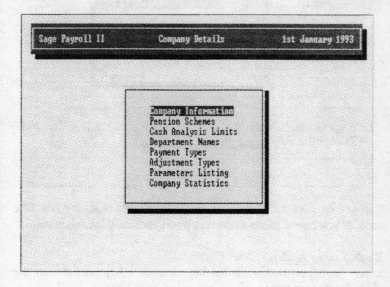

| Sage Payroll II | Company Details | 1st January 1993 |

Company Information
Pension Schemes
Cash Analysis Limits
Department Names
Payment Types
Adjustment Types
Parameters Listing
Company Statistics

Company Information

When you select Company Information you will see this screen:

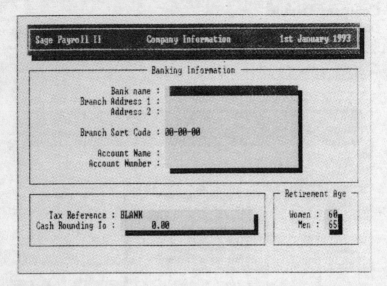

This screen asks for basic data about the firm's bank account (the account you intend to pay the wages from), including the following:

Bank Name / Address / Sort Code

Enter the information, remembering to enter a hyphen between the digits for the sort code.

Account Name / Number

Enter the details of these.

Tax Reference

Your tax district and reference number (this will be on correspondence from the Inland Revenue and on the tax forms you receive).

Cash Rounding To

You can ask the program to round to the nearest (e.g. ten pence).

Retirement Age

This figure can be altered to the specific figures for your company.

ESC when finished.

Pension Schemes

You can have up to ten different company pension schemes operating at any one time.

The screen is divided into three different sections, the left section dealing with Employer pension rates, the middle part of the screen with Employee pension rates and the far right with Contracted out schemes.

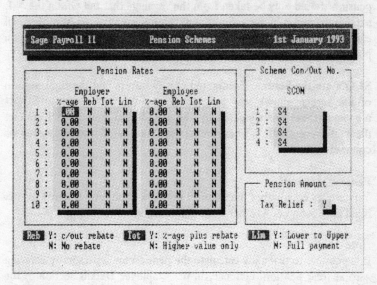

The information on the screen is brief so some explanation is needed.

The left two parts of the screen contain common data for both the employer and employee.

% - age

You should enter the exact percentage that is to be paid towards the pension from the earnings of the employee and the percentage payable by the employee.

Reb

You can enter **Y** or **N** here. If you enter **Y** then the program will calculate the minimum contribution for a contracted out pension scheme (i.e. the N.I. contracted out rebate).

Tot
Again you can enter **Y** or **N**. If you enter **Y** then the program will total the two previous values (%-age and Reb). Otherwise the program will use the higher of the two values.

Lim
This asks for you to decide whether the percentage contribution to the pension should only be taken from the earnings that fall within the N.I. maximum and minimum limits. If you answer **Y** to this then all earnings that fall outside those limits will be ignored for pension purposes.

SCON are the Scheme Contracted Out Numbers and the right section of the screen allows you to enter up to fourteen separate SCON numbers (these are allocated by the DHSS and you should contact them if necessary). These must be entered if the employee is contracted out.

Pension Amount
You are asked whether the Pension payment should be allowed for tax relief purposes, i.e. whether it should be taxed.

Note
It is possible to manually calculate the pension for a person by entering zero as their pension reference (in the Employee Details section of the program).

ESC when finished.

Cash Analysis Limits
If you wish you can decide on the **minimum** quantities of each type of currency, you can also exclude any type of large bank note (£10 or over) from being used by entering 9999 into the relevant field, the program will convert this to the symbol **- -**.

If you leave the default settings then the program will attempt to calculate the minimum quantities of each type of currency to be used.

The screen looks like this:

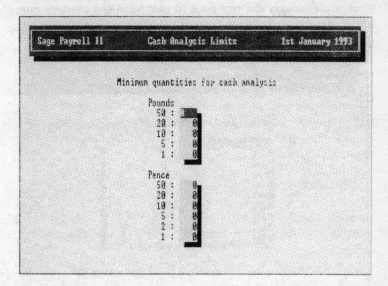

When you have finished just **ESC** back to the previous menu.

Department Names

If your firm uses a departmental structure then you can enter up to 99 separate departments. This can be useful for example to calculate the wage costs for each section of your business. These have to be entered again even if you have already created a departmental structure for the accounts.

When finished **ESC** back to the previous menu.

Payment Types

Most businesses pay different rates (if only basic and overtime rates). SAGE payroll enables you to have up to 10 different pay types.

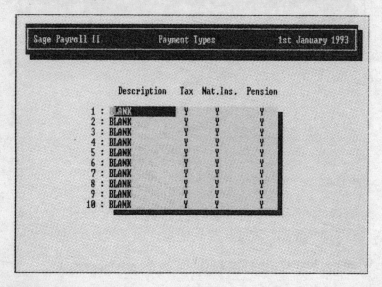

Description

You enter text here to describe the type of payment.

Tax / Nat Ins / Pension

You must enter **Y** or **N** in these columns. If you enter **Y** (the default) this means that those deductions will be made from that type of payment.

When finished **ESC** back to the previous menu.

Adjustment Types

At this point you can decide upon any pre or post tax adjustments you want to make to the pay for your employees. The screen is shown below:

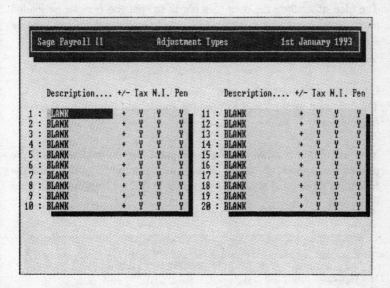

You can define up to twenty different adjustments to a person's pay (you select the specific adjustment for each employee when you add the employee to the payroll). The kinds of adjustments you may need to make are deductions for union membership, charitable payments, etc. The columns contain the following data:

Description
The name of the adjustment (whatever you wish to call it).

+ / -
Whether the adjustment is to be added or taken away from the pay.

Tax / N.I. / Pen
You have to answer **Y** or **N** to each of these. If you answer **Y** then the adjustment is made before tax is calculated.

When you have finished **ESC** back to the previous menu.

Parameters Listing

This selection allows you to print out the details you have entered for Company Details and Government Parameters so you have a hard copy for your files (or you can view them on screen or send them to a file). The idea of sending the data to a file is so that the file can be loaded into a word processing program and edited as necessary or just kept on file to be looked at later.

Company Statistics

This selection enables you to produce statistical information about the firm's payroll.

You will first be asked whether you want the finished report to be printed onto paper, displayed on screen or printed to a file Then the following screen will appear if you select to display it (rather than print it):

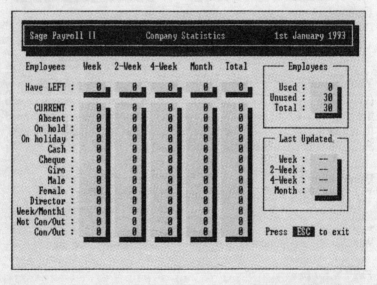

The information displayed in the report is as follows, the employees are firstly separated into the payment category, e.g. weekly, monthly, etc.

Have LEFT

This figure represents all those employees who have worked for you during the current tax year and have left during the year (and whom you have removed from the payroll).

Current

How many employees are still on the payroll.

Absent

This is a total number of those employees marked absent when the payroll was last run.

On holiday

Employees on holiday when the report is generated.

Cash / Giro / Cheque

How many employees are paid by each method.

Director / Male / Female

How many of each.

Week / Month 1

How many people have these tax codes.

Not Con / Out or Con / Out

SERPS is the State Earnings Related Pension Scheme and these rows show how many employees are contracted out of the SERPS scheme and how many are not.

When you have finished ESC back to the previous menu.

Employee Details

Whenever the details about your employees change then you will need to alter the Employee Details.

Select Employee Details from the menu and the following will appear on the screen:

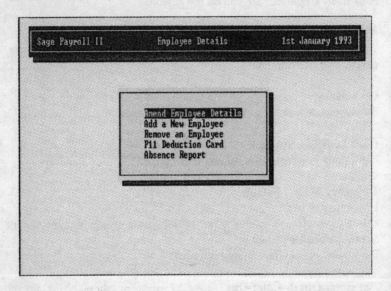

```
Sage Payroll II          Employee Details          1st January 1993




              Amend Employee Details
              Add a New Employee
              Remove an Employee
              P11 Deduction Card
              Absence Report
```

Add a New Employee

When you start using Payroll for the first time or when a new employee joins then you should choose this option to enter details about the person.

The first screen will ask how many new employees to add to your payroll. These will be added sequentially to the other numbers unless you specify otherwise (by starting from a number other than 1).

Then you will have to add the specific details about the employees.

This is the Personal Details screen (the first of four screens in this option):

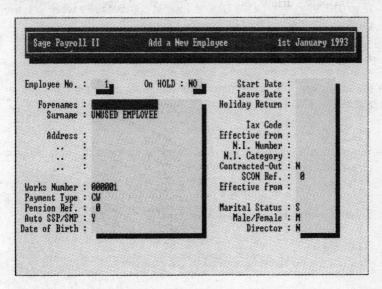

```
┌─────────────────────────────────────────────────────────────┐
│ Sage Payroll II          Add a New Employee      1st January 1993 │
│                                                               │
│   Employee No. :   1      On HOLD : NO      Start Date :      │
│                                             Leave Date :      │
│       Forenames :                        Holiday Return :     │
│        Surname : UNUSED EMPLOYEE                              │
│                                             Tax Code :        │
│         Address :                      Effective from :       │
│              .. :                         N.I. Number :       │
│              .. :                       N.I. Category :       │
│              .. :                     Contracted-Out : N       │
│                                           SCON Ref. : 0       │
│   Works Number : 000001                Effective from :       │
│   Payment Type : CW                                           │
│   Pension Ref. : 0                    Marital Status : S       │
│   Auto SSP/SMP : Y                       Male/Female : M       │
│   Date of Birth :                          Director : N       │
│                                                               │
└─────────────────────────────────────────────────────────────┘
```

Most of the data to be entered is specific to the person but some of the headings need explanation.

Payment Type

There are twelve different types of payment allowed for in the program:

CW Cash Weekly	C2 Cash Two-Weekly	C4 Cash Four-Weekly	CM Cash Monthly
QW Cheque Weekly	Q2 Cheque two-Weekly	Q4 Cheque Four-Weekly	QM Cheque Monthly
GW Giro Weekly	G2 Giro Two-Weekly	G4 Giro Four-Weekly	GM Giro Monthly

Pension Ref

This relates to the Pension Scheme details you entered under the Company Details (Pension Schemes) menu. If there is no pension scheme applicable to this employee enter 0 (zero).

Auto SSP/SMP

You enter **Y** or **N**. **Y** if you want to calculate the SSP (Statutory Sick Pay) or SMP (Statutory Maternity Pay) automatically.

Dates

All dates have to be entered as DDMMYY and zeros must be entered (e.g. 030793). The Leave Date is entered automatically when you use the Remove Employee option on the menu.

Holiday Return

This is automatically entered by the program when you begin to pay the employee after they have returned from an unpaid holiday or absence.

Tax Code

When entering this for the first time, or altering it, you will be prompted to confirm the amendment.

N.I.

Enter this without using any spaces.

NI Category

You can use **F3** to bring up a list of the categories.

SCON

This need only be entered if the employee is contracted out (and the employee belongs to an occupational pension scheme contracted out since 1/1/86.) You must use the pop-up table to enter this (**F3**).

Director

You must enter **Y** or **N**. **Y** means that the N.I. will be calculated on a cumulative basis.

At this point **do not ESC** but using the cursor keys continue onto the next screen where you enter more details.

You will see the following screen which is the Table Selection screen:

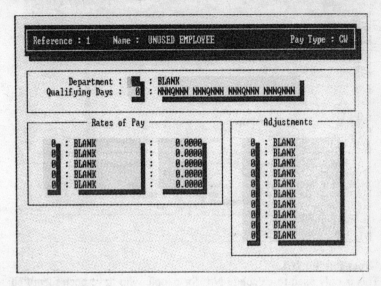

Department
If you have set up a department structure for your accounting records (Company Details - Department Names) then you should enter the relevant name here. Again you can use the **F3** key to pop up data.

Qualifying Days
You should have set up these within the Qualifying Days (Statutory Sick Pay) menu and you must enter one here (use the pop-up key **F3**).

Rates of Pay
Again you will have defined these within the Payment Types (Company Details) menu. Use the **F3** key to bring up the selection and then move the cursor to the third column and enter the amount.

Adjustments
These are set up by the Adjustment types (Company Details) menu. Use **F3** to pop-up the choices and **return**.

Use the cursor to move onto the next screen where the banking data will be entered.

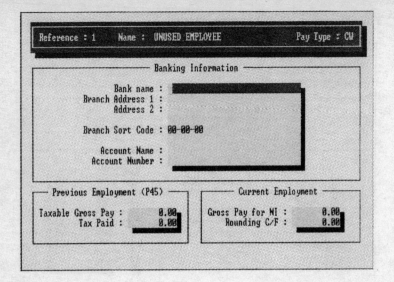

Gross Pay for N.I.
This is only used to calculate N.I. for people who have been identified to the program as directors and **must** only include current employment (i.e. in this employment before the payroll was computerised).

Rounding C/F
Here you can enter the rounding for the previous pay period.

Use the cursor keys to move onto the next screen which contains cumulative values and is used to enter values up to the date the payroll was computerised or the employee began working for you.

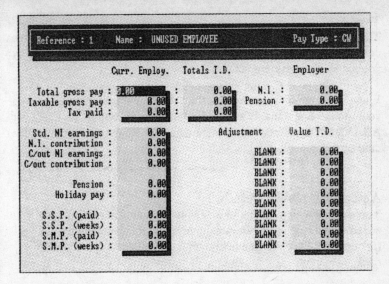

This screen enables you to enter the figures for the current tax year.
Most of these figures are taken from the employee's P11.

Please note that the details entered from the P45 section on the
previous screen appear again here.

Std N.I. earnings
This must not exceed the upper limit for N.I. contributions.

C/out N.I. earnings and C/out contribution
These are only to be entered if the employee is contracted out.

Pension
This means the total contributions for the year to date.

Holiday pay
Any money received by the person for the tax year to date.

SSP / SMP
Enter the amount and number of weeks for this tax year.

Total TD
This is in the middle column of the screen and will only differ from the current employment figures if the person was not been employed by you for all of the current tax year.

When you have finished entering the details for all the employees then you should **ESC** and **POST** them (there is an option to **EDIT** or **ABANDON** if you need to alter the details or have made a mess of the data entry).

Amend Employee Details
You use this option to alter or amend the details you entered when you added a new employee. Obviously this data can alter during a tax year (for example the employee may change their address or be given a pay rise).

You can alter any of the four data screens that you filled in when entering the new employee details. The Full Details option lets you alter all the screens or you can choose any of the individual screens.

The options are:

Full Details
Personal Details
Table Selections
Bank / P45 Information
Cumulative Values

After you enter the numbers of the employees you want to alter, you make the changes and when you have finished entering the data, you should **ESC** and **POST** the entries.

Removing an Employee

When an employee leaves you select this option to remove them from the payroll.

Remember that the date has to be entered in DDMMYY form.

After filling in the details, **return** and you will be asked to confirm that the details are correct and if they are, the employee's details will be removed from the payroll and the P45 and P11 will be produced.

P11 Deduction Card

You can produce a P11 deduction card for any or all of the employees by selecting this option and following through the question on the screen.

Absence Report

A very useful option, this enables you to print or view a report on an employee's absences. To do this you need to select the Absence Report option and answer the question displayed on the screen. The screen is very similar to the one shown above for the P11 report.

Statutory Sick Pay

As employers have to pay the SSP for their employees for a number of weeks, the program contains a section calculating SSP. The first screen you will see (after selecting Statutory Sick Pay from the main Payroll menu) is:

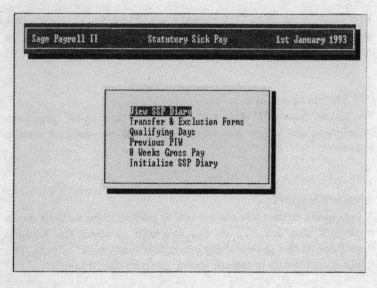

We will investigate each of these.

8 Weeks Gross Pay

When beginning to calculate the SSP for an employee, you should select this option first, followed directly by the Initialise SSP Diary option.

After entering the numbers of the employees you are interested in, you will get this screen which shows the average weekly earnings of an employee for the last 8 weeks. This is important as the average must exceed the N.I. lower earnings limit for the employee to qualify for SSP.

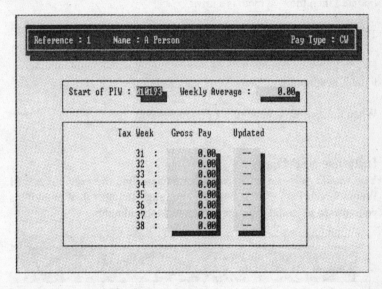

The data shown on the screen includes.

Start of PIW

This is the first day that the employee is absent (the absence should not be linked to any other absence). You can alter the date from the one shown.

Weekly Average

This is the average gross pay as calculated by the program from the data you have entered previously.

Tax Week
Based upon the date you have entered for the Start of PIW, these are the 8 weeks previous to this date.

Gross Pay
This is entered by the program unless the payroll has not been updated in which case you need to enter it manually.

Updated
The date that the payroll records were updated, if they have not been updated then the -- symbol is shown.

The following function keys can be used:

F9   previous record
F10   next record

When finished **ESC** back to the previous menu.

Initialise SSP Diary

You should only use this menu **after** having used the previous one (8 Weeks Gross Pay). After entering the range (numbers) of employees you wish to enter data for, the screen will look like this.

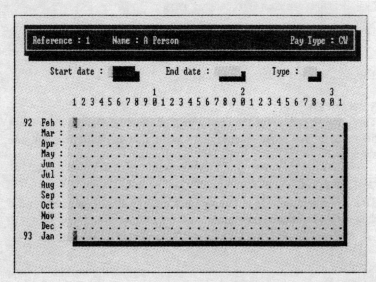

This screen is used to enter the previous absences of the employees.

Start Date
The first day the employee was absent.

End Date
The date the employee ceased to be off work (normally the day before returning to work), or the system date if the illness is continuing.

Type
You have a choice here:

A   absent
W   withheld (if you want to withhold the SSP for some reason).
      a day at work

When you have entered these you will be asked if you want to **Block Fill.** If you answer **Yes** then the diary is automatically filled between the dates you have entered.

To manually enter the data (rather than block fill), press **F3.** Then move the cursor to the required day and enter **A** or **W** and press **return**. Repeat this as necessary.

The following function keys can be used:

F7   the quick reference key (use this to check the details are correct)
F9   previous record
F10   next record

When finished **ESC** back to the previous menu.

Correcting Mistakes in the SSP Diary
Unfortunately you cannot edit directly, you have to select the Previous PIW option from the menu and reset the fields to zero and then edit the SSP diary again.

View SSP Diary

You will be asked to enter the number of the employees you wish to view the data for, the screen is very similar to that for Initialise SSP Diary. The data shown is for the preceding twelve months.

Remember that the pay type was entered by you when you added the employee to the payroll, the codes are:

CW	Cash Weekly	C2	cash Two-Weekly	C4	Cash Four-Weekly	CM	Cash Monthly
QW	Cheque Weekly	Q2	Cheque two-Weekly	Q4	Cheque Four-Weekly	QM	Cheque Monthly
GW	Giro Weekly	G2	Giro Two-Weekly	G4	Giro Four-Weekly	GM	Giro Monthly

Other data that will be displayed on the form are:

.	Normal Attendance	X	Qualifying Day	x	Provisional Qualifying Day
W	SSP Payment not paid	P	SSP paid for this day	p	Provisional Payment of SSP
A	Unpaid Day's Off Work				
=	Non-Qualifying Day (in a period of illness)			-	Provisional Non-Qualifying Day

Provisional payments are where the payroll has not been updated (although the absence periods have been entered).

The following function keys can be used (when finished **ESC** back to the previous menu):

F9 previous record
F10 next record

Transfer & Exclusion Forms

You may need to issue these forms to certain of your employees, and this section of the program will produce a report listing those employees who require one or other of the forms.

Transfer Forms

These must be issued to employees who will be claiming State Benefit after the SSP paid by the employer runs out. The forms must be issued well before the end of the period ends (check with the I.R. for the latest rules).

Exclusion Forms

These should be given to any employees who are to be excluded from SSP.

Qualifying Days (for SSP)

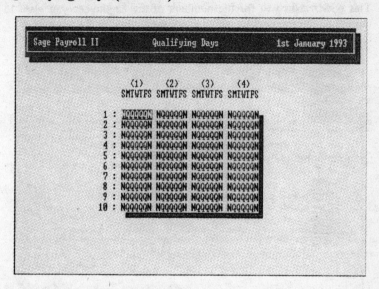

This screen is divided into four weeks (the four columns), each weekly heading showing the days of the week.

There are ten different weekly patterns that can be defined by using **Q** to represent a qualifying day and **N** for a non-qualifying day.

To alter the default patterns simply overtype it and press the **enter** or **return** key.

You can move the patterns around by pressing the **Pg Up** or **Pg Dn** keys and then selecting **Right** or **Left** to move the pattern to the left or right of the present position.

Press **ESC** when finished to return to the previous menu.

Previous PIW

This option asks you for the numbers of the employees you want to display on the screen, you will then see the following:

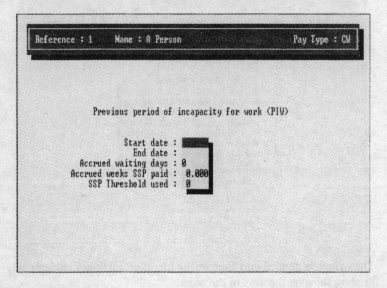

PIW means Period of Incapacity from Work and this screen shows the previous PIW for an employee.

The data is as follows:

Start date

The start date of the last PIW is shown here (or the start date of a continuing period of PIW).

End date

The end date of the previous PIW (or the system date if the PIW is ongoing).

Accrued waiting days

The number of accrued waiting days since the employee went sick.

Accrued weeks SSP paid

How many weeks (including part weeks) SSP has been paid for the latest PIW.

SSP Threshold used

Whatever threshold applies to this employee (see the Government Parameters section of the program).

The following function keys can be used:

F9   previous record
F10   next record

When finished **ESC** back to the previous menu.

Statutory Maternity Pay

After selecting this option, you will be asked to choose either:

Initialise SMP Dates
8 Weeks Gross Pay

We will look at each of these.

Initialise SMP Dates

This is the initial screen which appears after you have entered the numbers of the employees you want to deal with.

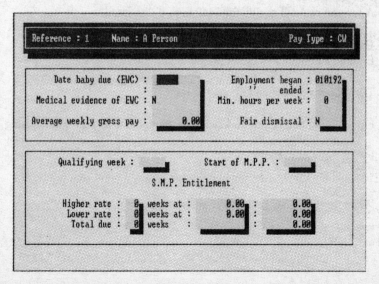

The data to be entered includes.

Medical evidence of EWC
The EWC is the date the baby is due and there should be documentary evidence, for example a maternity certificate. If there is no evidence then after 13 weeks of MPP a warning message will appear to this effect.

Average weekly gross pay
There are two methods of calculating this, automatically and manually:

Automatically Press the **F3** key and the program will calculate the last 8 weeks average.

Manually Enter the figure you have calculated.

Employment began
This is entered by the program.

Employment ended
Enter the date that maternity leave starts.

Min. hours per week
The figure for a normal week of employment.

Fair dismissal
A woman can still qualify for SMP even if dismissed.

Qualifying week
Entered automatically by the program.

The following function keys can be used:

F3   the quick reference key which produces a display summarising the SMP
F9   previous record
F10   next record

When finished **ESC** back to the previous menu.

8 Weeks Gross Pay

The same screens and data appear here as within the SSP option earlier.

Processing Payroll

You choose this option to actually carry out the weekly or monthly payroll. The screen is shown below (which is shown in total after you have agreed the initial data and hit the **return** key).

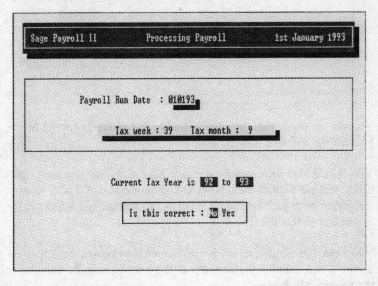

If you answer **Y** to the question at the bottom, the display changes to this.

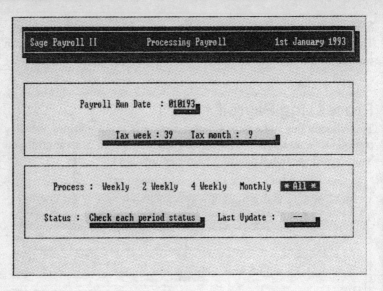

Sage Payroll II   Processing Payroll   1st January 1993

Payroll Run Date : 010193

Tax week : 39   Tax month : 9

Process : Weekly   2 Weekly   4 Weekly   Monthly   * All *

Status : Check each period status   Last Update :   —

You should check that the date shown on this screen is correct before proceeding, and alter it if you need to.

You should also (by moving the cursor keys to the left and then right) check that the various periods are OK to process. Do this by moving the cursor onto each one and if it is OK, a message will appear in the Status box to that effect.

When the data on this screen is satisfactory then **return** onto the next screen which asks for the numbers of the employees to be included in the payroll calculations.

A question will also appear at the bottom of the screen asking whether to clear the payments file.

If you answer **Y** then the payments file which contains the details on the last payroll run will be cleared of data.

You should only answer **Y** if the amounts paid to most employees differ from pay run to pay run. The idea is that if they are the same then they will not have to be entered again (in the Enter Payments screen, of which more later).

The following menu will now appear:

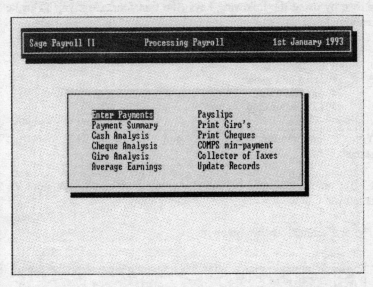

From this screen you have to select one of the menu options, which are explained below.

Enter Payments

This consists of two screens, which are shown on the following pages. From these two screens several related screens can be called by using the **F3** key. The screens that can be called up are the:

Personal Details	Table Selections	Banking Information
Cumulative Values	P11 Deduction Card	SSP Diary
SMP Dates	Holiday Pay Entry	

Each of these can be called after selecting the relevant field within the Enter Payments screen and then pressing the **F3** key.

The screens above can also be called up from anywhere within the first screen by using the following keys (the first four allow you to make changes to the data):

E Employee Details
T Table Selections
B Banking Information
C Cumulative Values
P P11 Deduction Card

You can also use the **T** key to bring up the relevant Table Selection screen.

F7 (the quick reference key) will also bring up summary data about the employee.

The first screen is shown below:

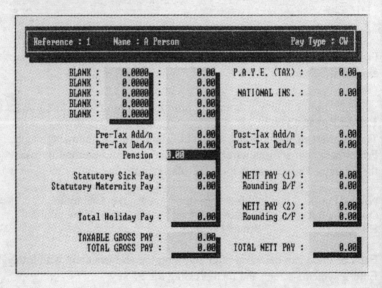

In the second screen are the adjustments to the pay and if this is the first time of use for an employee then you will have to enter the amounts, if this is not the first time then the amounts will have been entered by the program.

In the **ANP** column, you will see a three character reference, either **+YY**, **-YY**, **+YN**, **-YN**, **-NY** and so on (Y means yes, N means No). These come from the entries in the Adjustment Types (Company Details) menu.

A   stands for Addition / Deduction
N   for National Insurance
P   for Pension

Thus **+YY** means add the adjustment to both National Insurance and Pension.

Enter or alter the figures as necessary and **ESC** back to the previous menu.

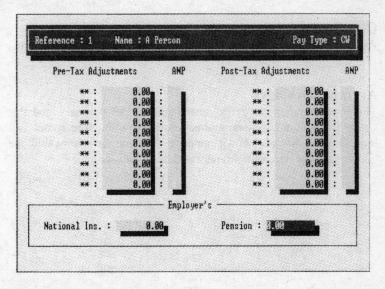

Finally in this option the following keys can be used to move around the employees:

F9   previous record
F10   next record

When finished **ESC** back to the previous menu.

Payments Summary

This option displays a summary of the payments and can be sent to the printer, to the screen or can be stored in a file for later use.

Cash Analysis

This gives a breakdown of the cash making up each pay-packet (as defined within the Company Details option).

Cheques Analysis

Produces a report on the cheque payments to employees paid by cheque (rather than by cash).

Giro Analysis

As cheques but where the payments are made through the Giro system.

Average Earnings

The program calculates average earnings for SSP purposes, and this option lets you display this information if you wish. The screen will look like the example shown opposite after you have answered the questions about which employees and dates to include.

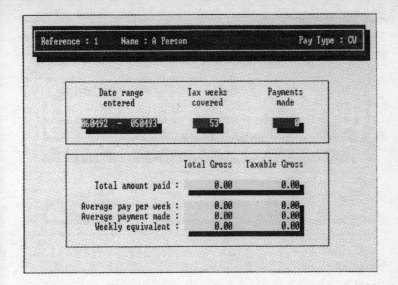

Payslips / Print Giros / Print Cheques

You can print, view on screen or print to file the pay-slips, etc., for your employees.

The program is supplied with various templates (design of form) and you can alter these or design your own using the Stationery Layouts option within the program.

Comps Min-Payment

The report generated by this option shows the minimum payments to a COMPS (this means Contracted-Out Money Purchase Scheme).

Collector of Taxes

This will produce a report which will identify how much money you have to pay the Inland Revenue for the specified tax month, the report will look like this:

```
┌─────────────────────────────────────────────────────────┐
│  ┌───────────────────────────────────────────────────┐  │
│  │        Collector of Taxes (Monthly Payslip Returns) │  │
│  │                                                     │  │
│  │     Record of deductions from gross National Insurance │
│  │                                                     │  │
│  │            (1)       (2)        (3)       (4)       (5) │
│  │   Type    S.S.P.  NIC comp'n  S.M.P.  NIC comp'n  Total Ded. │
│  │   Weekly   0.00     0.00       0.00     0.00       0.00 │
│  │ 2 Weekly   0.00     0.00       0.00     0.00       0.00 │
│  │ 4 Weekly   0.00     0.00       0.00     0.00       0.00 │
│  │   Monthly  0.00     0.00       0.00     0.00       0.00 │
│  │                                                     │  │
│  │   Totals   0.00     0.00       0.00     0.00       0.00 │
│  └───────────────────────────────────────────────────┘  │
│                                                         │
│  ┌───────────────────────────────────────────────────┐  │
│  │ NIC compensation percentage   Employee range    Date range │
│  │  S.S.P.    S.M.P.                          W 060492 - 050493 │
│  │   7.00      7.00              1  -  30     M 060492 - 050493 │
│  └───────────────────────────────────────────────────┘  │
└─────────────────────────────────────────────────────────┘
```

Update Records

Finally this option adds all the new figures for your employees to the cumulative totals ready for the next pay run.

Once an employee's records have been updated they cannot be changed. Please check that all the data you have entered is correct before updating the files. You can do this by checking the screens or by printing out the various reports and scrutinising these very carefully.

Always create a pre-update backup on a floppy disc before actually updating the file and write the date on this and keep it in a safe place.

The screen is shown below:

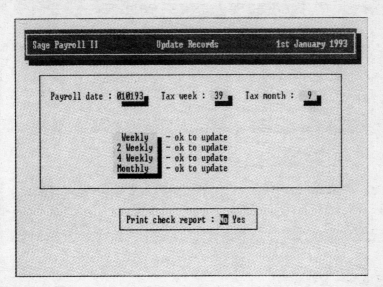

| Sage Payroll II | Update Records | 1st January 1993 |

Payroll date : **010193**␣ Tax week : **39**␣ Tax month : **9**␣

        Weekly␣ – ok to update
      2 Weekly␣ – ok to update
      4 Weekly␣ – ok to update
      Monthly␣ – ok to update

        Print check report : **No** Yes

STOCK CONTROL

This is optional, if you have purchased SAGE Financial Controller then it will be included or it can also be purchased separately. It is useful if you have a large amount or number of items of stock to keep track of or if you want to automate the production of Invoicing From Stock through the Sales Ledger (the stock levels will also be updated automatically).

The initial screen is shown below and sets out the various options within Stock Control.

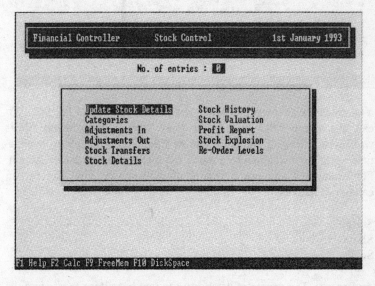

When setting up Stock Control for the first time, it is necessary to carry out a sequence of events as follows:

Set up the stock categories (Categories)
Update the stock details (Update Stock Details)
Enter the actual stock items (Adjustments In)

Categories

You enter the different types or categories of stock that you intend to carry. The list can be added to (or deleted from) at any stage. The entry screen looks like this:

107

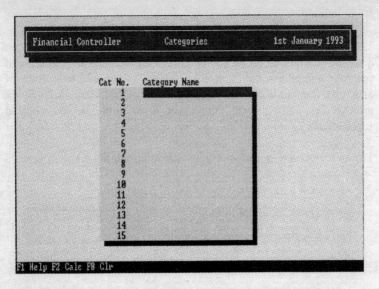

Cat No.   Category Name
1
2
3
4
5
6
7
8
9
10
11
12
13
14
15

F1 Help F2 Calc F8 Clr

You enter each category of stock and then **return** when finished. To exit this screen **ESC** back to the main Stock Control menu. It is worthwhile planning the categories of stock you are likely to need as time spent here will lead to a much more effective and usable system. For example if you are a retailer of clothes then you may set up categories such as:

Suits
Shirts
Socks

And so on. The degree of detail is up to you but please think carefully about what information you want from the system before starting to enter the categories (you can use up to a maximum of **90** different categories if you wish).

Update Stock Details

This is the section where you enter the actual details of the stock (NOT the number of items but details about the items). The entry screen is shown opposite.

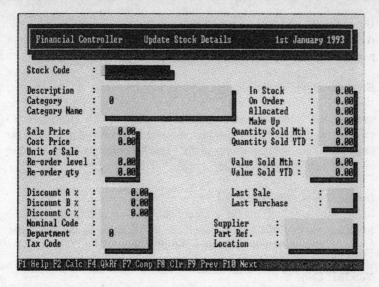

```
Stock Code        :

Description       :                    In Stock      :    0.00
Category          :  0                 On Order      :    0.00
Category Name     :                    Allocated     :    0.00
                                       Make Up       :    0.00
Sale Price        :    0.00            Quantity Sold Mth :  0.00
Cost Price        :    0.00            Quantity Sold YTD :  0.00
Unit of Sale      :
Re-order level    :    0.00            Value Sold Mth :    0.00
Re-order qty      :    0.00            Value Sold YTD :    0.00

Discount A %      :    0.00            Last Sale      :
Discount B %      :    0.00            Last Purchase  :
Discount C %      :    0.00
Nominal Code      :                    Supplier       :
Department        :  0                 Part Ref.      :
Tax Code          :                    Location       :
```

F1 Help F2 Calc F4 QkRf F7 Comp F8 Clr F9 Prev F10 Next

Some of the data will automatically appear, the data you need to enter
is:

Stock Code
This can be any mix of numbers and alphabetic characters you want (up
to 16 characters long).

I suggest you keep it as short and simple as possible as you will not
want to keep looking up the codes but will be able to commit the most
used codes to memory if they are short and easy to remember.

Description
This is any text which you enter to describe the item.

Category
This will default to 1, but you can alter it to the actual category number
you want (and when you have done this the Category Name will
automatically change).

Sale Price / Cost Price
You can only enter the Sale Price on this screen, you enter the cost
price when you enter new stock (Adjustments In).

Unit of Sale

A text entry noting the number of items normally sold together (e.g. a pair of shoes).

Re-order level / Re-order qty

You can (if you wish) enter figures here for the re-order level (the quantity left when you need to order new stock). It is possible to calculate mathematically the optimum re-order level (your accountant can work it out for you if you wish). The Re-order qty is the number of that item you normally order.

Discount A% (B% and C%)

It is possible to set up three discounts, any of which can then be automatically applied to any order. You are not tied to these and can give any discount to any order if you want to manually.

Nominal Code

This is the Nominal Code for the sale (i.e. it should be a Sales code). If you enter the code then it will be automatically posted when the invoice is produced.

Department

You need to enter this if you have set up a departmental structure.

Tax Code

Entering this means that the correct tax code will be entered onto the invoice when it is produced.

Supplier

The supplier's code (which you created when you set up the Purchase Ledger).

Part Ref

Up to 16 characters to identify the part number of the item (normally the supplier's part number).

Location

Again a 16 character code which can be used to identify where the item is stored (often this is termed the bin number as stock items were traditionally held in bins).

After the Location is entered (or passed over as you only have to enter it if you want to), if you press **F7** the screen changes to that shown below:

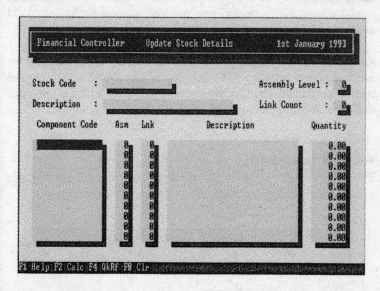

This is the **Components Assembly** screen and is totally optional and you only need to use it if you want to identify the particular components you use to make up an item (useful in a manufacturing business among others).

In previous versions of SAGE a similar screen would appear automatically.

Some explanation is needed here.

Assembly Level
This is a number which represents how near to being complete the item is in terms of the units making it up. If all the items making up the stock item are complete in themselves then the level will be 1.

Link Count
The number of other stock items which make reference to this item (i.e. which include it in their assembly details).

Component Code / Description / Quantity
You need to enter the code of each item used to make the stock item along with the number of units of that item to be used. The description should appear automatically once you have entered the code. **ASM** and **Lnk** are the assembly level and link count for each component.

When you have finished entering these details **ESC** back to the previous screen and then **ESC** and you can then **POST** the item to the stock records, **ABANDON** the entry or you can **DELETE** the stock item from the records.

Adjustments In
This is used where you want to enter stock into the records. It is also used to enter the opening stock. The screen is shown below:

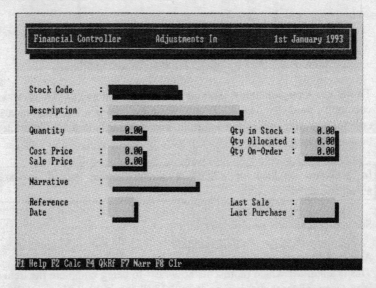

All you need to enter here is the Stock Code and the Quantity, all the other data is displayed automatically for you. When you have finished entering the data **ESC** and **POST**.

Adjustments Out

The same as Adjustments In except that stock is going out. You would use this for items that have been destroyed or lost or sold without going through the automatic production of invoices (for example where you have used Free Text invoicing).

Stock Transfers

The same screen as for the Adjustments. The Stock Transfer option is used to make up a stock item from its component parts. The **Qty Make-Up** figure must be greater than zero and you can only enter a figure up to the Qty Make Up figure as this represents the maximum number of items that can be made up from the stock levels that exist.

After you have entered the quantity you need, the items making up the (components) will be deducted from the relevant stock levels.

Stock Details

You can display stock details by choosing this option, you will be asked to choose whether you want a report organised by Category or Stock Codes and then the upper and lower codes you are interested in and whether you want the report on screen, printed or written to file (for later use). If you just return through the questions you will get a report of all categories of stock displayed on the screen.

Stock History

Another type of report that SAGE can generate, this time instead of details about the stock items, a history of (chosen or all) stock items can be displayed.

```
AI adjustments in      MI movements in       GI goods in
AO adjustments out     MO movements out      GO goods out
```

Stock Valuation

You can display (or print) a summary of the values of your stock either by category or by stock codes. Again you can include all the codes or select specific ranges of codes.

Profit Report

A report showing the differences between the cost of items and the sale prices. You can show this for all the stock or for selected items, and for the current month or for the cumulative months.

Stock Explosion

A report is generated for all stock items that are made up of components showing what components each item is made up of.

Re-order Levels

A report detailing the stock items that need to be re-ordered (i.e. those stock items that have fallen below their re-order level).

SALES AND PURCHASE ORDER PROCESSING

This option lets you control your sales and purchase ordering. The difference between Sales and Purchase Order Processing is that the Sales Orders are processed through the Sales and Nominal ledgers but the Purchase option is not posted to the ledger so any posting will still have to be carried out manually. Both options update the stock records automatically though (you have to run the **Update Ledgers** option in the Sales Ledger Invoice Production to update the stock and the orders have to be processed for the purchases to update the stock).

After choosing the Sales Order Processing option you will be presented with the following screen:

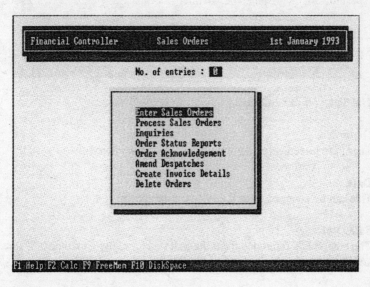

```
┌──────────────────────────────────────────────────────────────┐
│  Financial Controller        Sales Orders        1st January 1993 │
│                                                                │
│                      No. of entries : 0                        │
│                                                                │
│              ┌────────────────────────────────┐               │
│              │    Enter Sales Orders           │               │
│              │    Process Sales Orders         │               │
│              │    Enquiries                    │               │
│              │    Order Status Reports         │               │
│              │    Order Acknowledgement        │               │
│              │    Amend Despatches             │               │
│              │    Create Invoice Details       │               │
│              │    Delete Orders                │               │
│              └────────────────────────────────┘               │
│                                                                │
│ F1 Help F2 Calc F9 FreeMem F10 DiskSpace                       │
└──────────────────────────────────────────────────────────────┘
```

Dealing with these in sequence, firstly:

Enter Sales Orders

The initial screen looks like this:

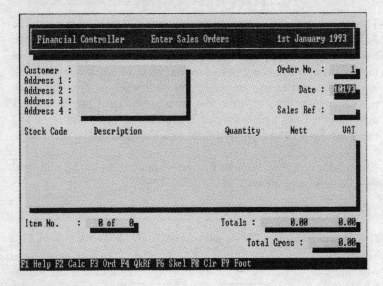

```
┌──────────────────────────────────────────────────────────────────┐
│  Financial Controller      Enter Sales Orders      1st January 1993 │
│                                                                      │
│  Customer  :                               Order No. :        1      │
│  Address 1 :                                                         │
│  Address 2 :                                 Date :   1193           │
│  Address 3 :                                                         │
│  Address 4 :                               Sales Ref :              │
│                                                                      │
│  Stock Code    Description           Quantity     Nett      VAT     │
│                                                                      │
│                                                                      │
│                                                                      │
│                                                                      │
│                                                                      │
│  Item No.  :    0 of   0              Totals :     0.00     0.00    │
│                                                                      │
│                                        Total Gross :        0.00    │
│                                                                      │
│ F1 Help F2 Calc F3 Ord F4 QkRf F6 Skel F8 Clr F9 Foot              │
└──────────────────────────────────────────────────────────────────┘
```

The data you can enter is:

Order No.
These are incremented automatically but can be altered if you wish to.

Date
This can be changed from the system date shown.

Sales Ref
The customer's reference from the Sales Ledger, the Customer's Name and Address should then automatically appear.

If you enter an unknown reference then SAGE will ask you if it is a new reference and then you will be able to enter the customer details without having to go to the Sales Ledger screen.

If you press the key **F3** then the following screen will be displayed which lets you enter more details about the transaction.

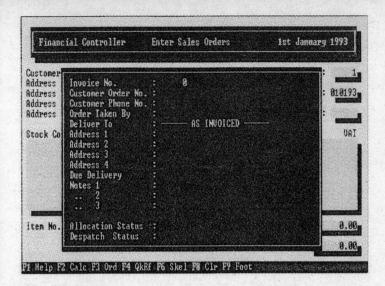

```
Customer                                                          :      1
Address   Invoice No.          :        0
Address   Customer Order No.   :                                  : 010193
Address   Customer Phone No.   :
Address   Order Taken By       :
          Deliver To           : ——— AS INVOICED ———
Stock Co  Address 1            :                                     VAT
          Address 2            :
          Address 3            :
          Address 4            :
          Due Delivery         :
          Notes 1              :
          ..   2               :
          ..   3               :
item No.  Allocation Status    :                                   0.00
          Despatch  Status     :
                                                                   0.00
```

F1 Help F2 Calc F3 Ord F4 QkRf F6 Skel F8 Clr F9 Foot

Order Taken By
The name of the salesperson taking the order or any other text you wish to enter (this can be used for analysis purposes using the Report Generator so that you can create a report showing how each salesperson has done).

Due Delivery
The delivery date.

Customer Order No.
The customer's reference for the order.

Allocation Status / Despatch Status
This shows whether the items have been fully, partly or not allocated (or despatched).

F9 will bring the following screen which lets you enter the footer details for the order.

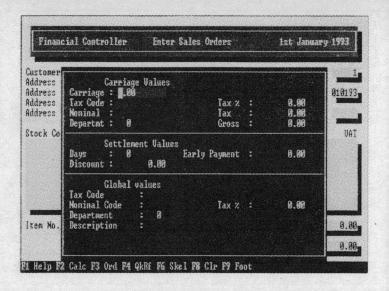

Customer
Address
Address   Carriage Values
Address   Carriage : 0.00
Address   Tax Code :   Tax % :   0.00
           Nominal :   Tax   :   0.00
           Departmt :   0   Gross :   0.00
Stock Co
                Settlement Values
           Days   :   0   Early Payment :   0.00
           Discount :   0.00

                Global values
           Tax Code   :
           Nominal Code :   Tax % :   0.00
           Department :   0
Item No.   Description :

F1 Help F2 Calc F3 Ord F4 QkRf F6 Skel F8 Clr F9 Foot

1
010193
VAT
0.00
0.00

Version 4 screens are slightly different and appear automatically in sequence.

Process Sales Orders

After entering the Sales Order, you have to process it. After selecting this option simply enter the Upper and Lower Order No. and whether you want to process Automatically or Manually (Manually allows you to allocate, unallocate, cancel, etc.).

It is not possible to despatch the items until an invoice has been created.

Enquiries

This option lets you look at the data you have entered.

Order Status Reports

This option gives you information about the status of your orders, there are three types:

Back Orders
This is an order or part order that has not been processed for a variety of reasons (e.g. lack of stock).

Outstanding Orders
An order that has been allocated stock but has not been despatched.

Despatched Orders
Orders that have been completed and despatched (this can include cancelled orders).

For each of these you will be asked for the Upper and Lower Order No., and the Range of dates you are interested in.

Order Acknowledgement

This prints out an order acknowledgement for you to send to your customers.

Amend Despatches

This option lets you alter the amount of items you have recorded as being despatched.

Create Invoice Details

You can use this option to pass data to the Invoice Production Option within the Sales Ledger but only if the order is partly or fully allocated (and only the allocated items will be transferred). A report is produced detailing the order items that have been processed.

Delete Orders

You will be asked for the Order Numbers you wish to delete.

Purchase Order Processing

This follows the same procedures as Sales Order Processing and is a mirror image (in the same way the Sales Ledger and Purchase Ledgers are mirrors of each other).

REPORT GENERATOR

Within SAGE you can create many different reports based upon the data you have entered. These reports display the data in different ways. You can use the existing report layouts or you can create your own layouts.

Using the Existing Reports

After selecting Report Generator from the main menu, you will see the following screen:

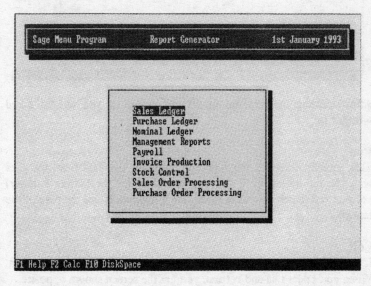

Sage Menu Program   Report Generator   1st January 1993

Sales Ledger
Purchase Ledger
Nominal Ledger
Management Reports
Payroll
Invoice Production
Stock Control
Sales Order Processing
Purchase Order Processing

F1 Help F2 Calc F10 DiskSpace

Each of these options has several reports you can use immediately.

Using the Sales Ledger option (as an example) you can select different report layouts (which can be displayed on screen or printed to file or onto paper). The following screen shows the Sales Ledger reports:

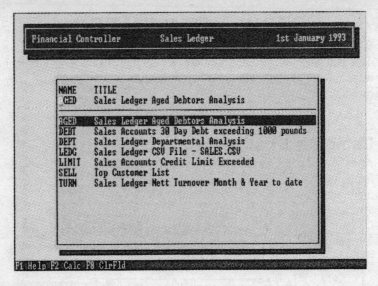

```
NAME    TITLE
 GED    Sales Ledger Aged Debtors Analysis

AGED    Sales Ledger Aged Debtors Analysis
DEBT    Sales Accounts 30 Day Debt exceeding 1000 pounds
DEPT    Sales Ledger Departmental Analysis
LEDG    Sales Ledger CSV File - SALES.CSV
LIMIT   Sales Accounts Credit Limit Exceeded
SELL    Top Customer List
TURN    Sales Ledger Nett Turnover Month & Year to date
```

F1 Help F2 Calc F8 ClrFld

After selecting the required report and **return**ing you will be asked whether to:

Run

This actually compiles the report by merging the data from the files with the report layout. You will be asked for the (lower / upper) account references you want to include in the report and the date of the report.

Edit

If you want to alter any of the existing reports you can edit them. When you select this and **return**, you get the screen shown opposite.

Print

You can print a copy of the format of the report.

Delete

If you want to you can delete a report.

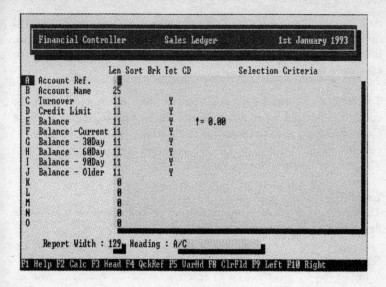

```
              Len Sort Brk Tot CD            Selection Criteria
A  Account Ref.
B  Account Name    25
C  Turnover        11        Y
D  Credit Limit    11        Y
E  Balance         11        Y      != 0.00
F  Balance -Current 11       Y
G  Balance - 30Day 11        Y
H  Balance - 60Day 11        Y
I  Balance - 90Day 11        Y
J  Balance - Older 11        Y
K                   0
L                   0
M                   0
N                   0
O                   0

    Report Width : 129  Heading : A/C
F1 Help F2 Calc F3 Head F4 QckRef F5 VarHd F8 ClrFld F9 Left F10 Right
```

Altering the Fields

To alter the format of the report, move the cursor to the row you want to alter or add to, press **F4** to bring up a list of possible fields, move the cursor within this list to the one you want and **return**. You have 52 possible rows of which the first few already contain fields (which you can replace if you want).

When you press **F4** you are given a list of the available fields which are shown below for reference.

Account Ref.	Balance - 30 Day	Payment Ref.
Account Name	Balance - 60 Day	Amount - Paid
Address 1	Balance - 90 Day	Amount - Due
Address 2	Balance - Older	Tax Code
Address 3	Transaction No.	Tax Percentage
Address 4	Type (Long)	Paid (Yes/No)
Telephone Number	Type (Short)	Age of Trans.
Contact Name	Nominal A/C	Next Trans. A/C
Analysis Code	Department No.	Next Trans. N/C
Discount Code	Department Name	Report Date
Last Inv. Date	Transaction Date	Date From
First Trans. No.	Transaction Ref.	Date To
Last Trans. No.	Details	Calculated field
Credit Limit	Amount - Nett	Remove field
Turnover	Amount - Tax	Insert field
Balance	Amount - Gross	
Balance -Current	Payment Date	

Any of these can be inserted into the report and so can Calculated fields (this allows you to make calculations within a field (e.g. F*.10), this works out 10% of the value in field F wherever you put the calculated field).

To create a calculated field you need to select a row by moving the cursor to the row letter and then use **F4** to list the fields. Choose Calculated Field and then enter the calculation.

The other columns on the screen are:

Len
The length of the field, unless you need to you can leave this as the default (which is entered automatically).

Sort
You are able to sort the data by entering certain criteria here, you can define up to nine fields to include in the sort and you can set each field to be in ascending (**A**) or descending (**D**) order.

All you need to do is to enter between 1A or 1D in the primary field, 2A or 2D in the second field and so on up to 9A or 9D (if you so wish). The primary field is 1, the secondary field 2, etc. This means that the data will be sorted by field 1 (then within field 1 by field 2).

To give a simple example, if field 1 was (a person's) age then the data would be sorted into age order. If the secondary field was sex (M or F) then all the people of a specific age would be sorted into F(emale) first then M(ale). The sorted records would look like this:

```
primary        secondary

Age            Sex
34             F
34             F
34             M
40             F
40             M
40             M
```

Brk
You can make the report look more readable by using either:
L   this prints a blank line where the data changes in that field (e.g. age).
P   a new page is started when the data changes.

Tot
If you want the column to be totalled you should enter **Y**. You can also enter **T** which will produce sub-totals for each break.

CD
If you want any value to be shown as a credit, debit or as balance columns then you need to type either:

C (credit)	this displays all values of zero or greater
D (debit)	this displays values less than zero
S (balance)	totals the debit and credit values

Selection Criteria
In this column you can use logical and other operators (as you would in a spreadsheet). The following operators can be used:

Arithmetic Operators

=	equal to
!<	not equal to
<	less than
>	greater than
<=	less than or equal to
>=	greater than or equal to

For example you could enter into a field
>3000
and only those records that agreed with this would be included in the report.

Logical Operators
AND
OR

For example if you enter >3000   AND   <3500 only those records greater than 3000 and less than 3500 would be included.

There is a considerable difference between using AND and OR as logical operators (think about what would occur if you substituted OR in the above example).

Wild cards
SAGE supports the normal DOS wild cards, you can use:

*   to represent any number of characters
?   to represent a single character

For example =B* will list all those items beginning with the character
B. You should enter alphabetic characters as capitals, otherwise the
report generator will not accept them.

Looking for text
As well as the operators and wild cards described above you can search
for text within other text which you want to include or exclude from
the report. To do this you need to use the following:

$text   selects records containing the typed text
!$text   excludes records containing the typed text

For example $is if you want to look for all text that contains the
characters is

As you can see from the above, the text contains no spaces. If you
want to look for text that contains spaces then you need to enclose the
text within inverted commas. Obviously the text you are looking for
has to match the text you have typed.

When looking for text within text you do not use arithmetic operators,
but you can combine this search with arithmetic operators, e.g.

$ART   OR   =B*

This will look for all words containing the character string ART or any
words beginning with the letter B.

Print
This prints the format of the report so you can see the way it is made
up (for example if you want to edit it, you will have a hard copy to
refer to).

Delete
You can delete any report from the list.

Creating a Totally New Report

As you have seen, you can use the existing reports as they already exist or you can adapt them for your own purposes. It is also possible to create your own individualised reports from scratch. In fact it could be quicker to do this than to adapt existing report formats.

All you need to do is to choose the Report Generator menu and then the type of activity you want to create the report for, e.g. Sales Ledger reports.

Type a new name over the name the cursor is positioned over and **return**. Then choose EDIT, give it a title and **return**. You will be presented with a new report form to fill in. Use **F4** to bring up a list of fields you can use, select the field and **return.** Once you have chosen the fields then you carry on in the same way as for the existing forms (remember to save the new form if you are likely to want to use it again, the name will be added to the list of reports).

If you want to adapt one of the existing reports **and** keep the original then copy the file to a new name using the Utilities (DOS functions) option.

UTILITIES

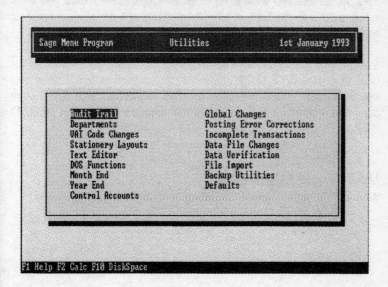

```
Sage Menu Program              Utilities              1st January 1993
```

```
  Audit Trail              Global Changes
  Departments              Posting Error Corrections
  VAT Code Changes         Incomplete Transactions
  Stationery Layouts       Data File Changes
  Text Editor              Data Verification
  DOS Functions            File Import
  Month End                Backup Utilities
  Year End                 Defaults
  Control Accounts
```

```
F1 Help F2 Calc F10 DiskSpace
```

Audit Trail

This is a list of all the transactions that have taken place (including journal entries). Its main function is to list the transactions sequentially so that you are able to see exactly what you have entered into your accounting records. They can also be used by auditors to check the correctness of your accounts.

After selecting this option you will be asked whether you want the data displayed on the screen or printed out or printed to a file (for later use).

The data displayed is in the order you entered it and each transaction is given a number and is identified as a particular type of transaction. The various types are shown below.

SI	sales invoice	SC	sales credit note	SR	sales receipt
PI	purchase invoice	PC	purchase credit note	PP	purchase payment
PA	purchase payment on account	PD	purchase discount		
CP	cash payment	CR	cash receipt		
JC	journal credit	JD	journal debit		
SA	sales payment on account	SD	sales discount		
BP	bank payment	BR	bank receipt		

The headings are similar to the other reports you have already seen.

Departments

This option lets you view a list of all the department names you have set up or to edit the list (i.e. alter it by changing a department name or adding a new department name).

You will be presented with several options asking you whether you want to display (look at) or edit (alter) the list, which departments you are interested in and whether to print or display the list. Any department numbers that you have not used are shown as UNUSED DEPARTMENT.

VAT Code Changes

After selecting this you will be presented with the following screen.

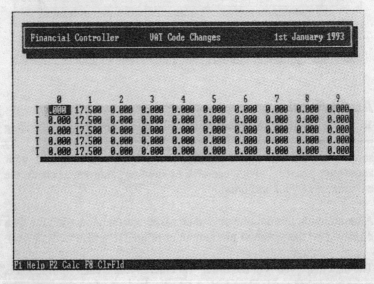

You have great flexibility within the program to set up many different tax codes (50 to be exact).

The default codes (the ones the program comes with) are:

T0   zero rated
T1   standard rate (at present 17.5%)
T9   non-VATable transactions

To alter a code (or letter) move the cursor onto the number and enter the new number then **return** (it is vital to return otherwise the alteration will not be accepted).

The tax codes set up are **T0** to **T9** (as can be seen from the screen), however you can change any of the **T**'s in the first column to any other character, thus giving you five ranges of code to use.

Stationery Layouts

You have the option within SAGE to alter various layouts for the forms that SAGE produces. The various options are shown below:

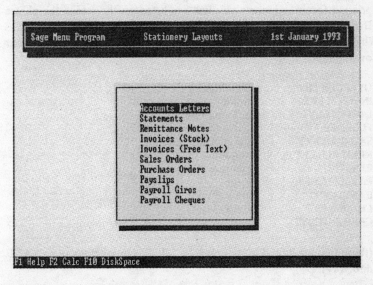

```
Sage Menu Program        Stationery Layouts        1st January 1993


                         Accounts Letters
                         Statements
                         Remittance Notes
                         Invoices (Stock)
                         Invoices (Free Text)
                         Sales Orders
                         Purchase Orders
                         Payslips
                         Payroll Giros
                         Payroll Cheques




F1 Help F2 Calc F10 DiskSpace
```

To display any of these, **return** on the chosen option and then **return** again to display the default layout.

The details shown can be adapted or customised to your own requirements by adding and deleting either text or the actual data fields.

To add a field move the cursor to the required position, press **F4** to bring up the list of possible fields, move the cursor to the field you want and **return**. The fields are highlighted in blue on the screen.

To remove an unwanted field, delete it by moving the cursor onto the field and use **F8** to delete it and **return**.

To alter text simply move the cursor over the text, delete it and replace it with your own text then **ESC** and **save** the amended file.

Please note that the actual display extents over three screens so you can only see part of it at any one time.

You can customise the layout to your own needs or you can start again and create a new layout and then save it under a new file name.

The layouts that come with the program are listed below. Often when printing forms or reports you will see listed on the screen the phrase INPUT (or OUTPUT) FILE. This is a reference to one of the forms (below). You can either use the form given or substitute one of your own design.

OVERDUE.LET	debt collection
INVOICE.LYT	invoice
INVTEXT.LYT	free form invoice
PUORDER.LYT	purchase order
SAORDER.LYT	sales acknowledgement
STATFREE.LYT	statement
REMITNC.LYT	remittance notes
PAYSLIP.LYT	payslip
BANKGIRO.LYT	bank giro credit
CHEQUE.LYT	payroll cheque layout
CHEQUNIT.LYT	cheque layout

(these files are stored in the company sub directory off the main SAGE directory).

If you want to alter them you may wish to copy them to another name so that the originals are still available to you (and then use the new versions to alter). To copy the files either use the DOS COPY command or the DOS FUNCTIONS within the SAGE program.

You can alter the name that appears on the top line, this will bring up the message NEW FILE, you can then create your own layout which you can save and re-use as necessary. Use the text editing keys to move around the document (see next page).

Text Editor

You can use the text editor to create your own forms and layouts rather than use or adapt the pre-set ones. The text editor works like a simple word processor (which is essentially what it is). To begin you need to type in a filename (either an existing one or a new one)

The main key strokes are.

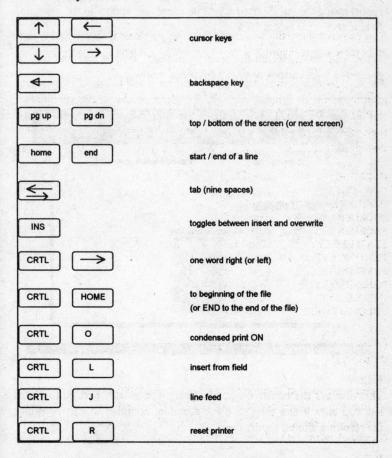

↑ ↓	← →	cursor keys
⬅		backspace key
pg up	pg dn	top / bottom of the screen (or next screen)
home	end	start / end of a line
⇤		tab (nine spaces)
INS		toggles between insert and overwrite
CRTL	⟶	one word right (or left)
CRTL	HOME	to beginning of the file (or END to the end of the file)
CRTL	O	condensed print ON
CRTL	L	insert from field
CRTL	J	line feed
CRTL	R	reset printer

When you have finished entering the text you **ESC** and are then asked if you want to **Save**, **Edit**, **Abandon** or **Print** the text.

DOS Functions

This option lets you use certain DOS (disk operating system) commands without leaving the program. This can be time saving and therefore convenient.

The screen will automatically show a listing of any reports you have printed to file while you have been using the ledgers. To choose a report move the cursor onto it and its name will appear in the Filename field above.

When you have selected the report you want, **return** and you will be presented with various options (described below):

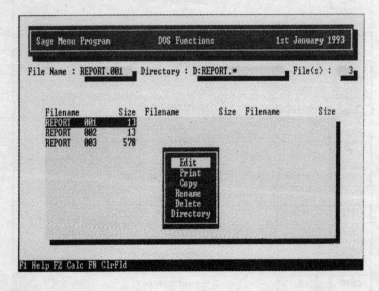

Edit
This displays the report on screen (using the in-built text editor) and lets you alter it and then save (or abandon, continue to edit or print) the resulting altered report.

Print
Use this to print the report.

Copy

If you choose this option a new field will appear below the original Fieldname and you will be asked for a New Name for the copied file. You will end up with two files, the original and the copy.

Rename

This operates in the same way as Copying except you end up with only one file.

Delete

If you do not need the file any more then you can delete it. Please be warned that once a file has been deleted it has gone.

Directory

By choosing this option you can alter the directory that is being used for the DOS Functions screen. All you need to do is to type in the new directory path and the type of file (you will need to know something about DOS paths and filenames to do this, for example to copy a stationery layout you may have to alter the directory to Company0*.lyt).

To use files other than report files, **return** and choose Directories and enter a new path, e.g. Company0*.*, then enter the file name or move the cursor over the required file.

Month End

At the end of each month there are special procedures that should be carried out so that the monthly accounts are correct.

The five items that can be adjusted for are:

Recurring Entries
Prepayments & Accruals
Depreciation
Stock
Create Month End Accounts

A couple of the screens are shown for reference, please note that the process is automatic so that once you have **return**ed then the process will take place.

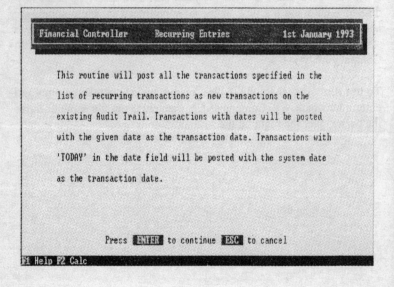

W A R N I N G

This routine will automatically zero the `QUANTITY` `SOLD` and `SALES VALUE` in each stock item for the current period ONLY!

Please ensure the following reports have been printed before proceeding with this routine.

```
STOCK HISTORY REPORT
STOCK VALUATION REPORT
STOCK PROFIT REPORT
```

Press `ENTER` to continue `ESC` to cancel

F1 Help F2 Calc F9 FreeMem F10 DiskSpace

Year End

This should be carried out at the end of your financial year to set up the accounts ready for the next year. Within this option you can adjust for three different types of transaction:

Accounts

The screen for this option is shown below:

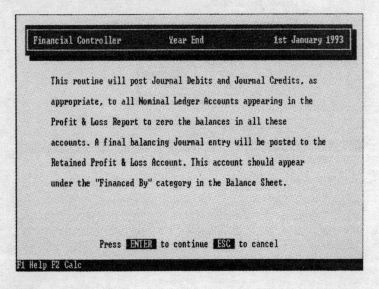

This routine will post Journal Debits and Journal Credits, as appropriate, to all Nominal Ledger Accounts appearing in the Profit & Loss Report to zero the balances in all these accounts. A final balancing Journal entry will be posted to the Retained Profit & Loss Account. This account should appear under the "Financed By" category in the Balance Sheet.

Press **ENTER** to continue **ESC** to cancel

F1 Help F2 Calc

Stock

The Stock screen is virtually the same as that shown above for the Month End procedures.

Payroll

Within this are four further options. The first three are reports and forms, the last is not and a warning message is shown on screen (and reproduced below).

P35 Year End Summary
P11 Deduction Form
P14/P60 Certificate
Clear Year-TD Totals

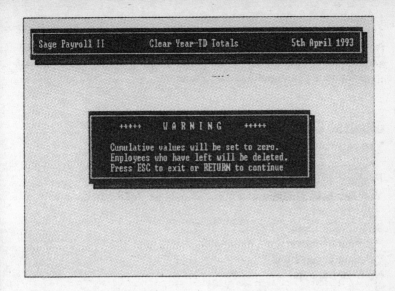

```
 Sage Payroll II        Clear Year-TD Totals        5th April 1993



                    +++++  W A R N I N G  +++++

                    Cumulative values will be set to zero.
                    Employees who have left will be deleted.
                    Press ESC to exit or RETURN to continue
```

Control Accounts

```
 Financial Controller     Control Accounts         1st January 1993



                    Debtors Control Account   : 1100
                    Creditors Control Account : 2100
                    Bank Account              : 1200
                    Bank Account Number 2     :
                    Bank Account Number 3     :
                    Bank Account Number 4     :
                    Bank Account Number 5     :
                    Cash Account              : 1230
                    Tax Control Account       : 2200
                    Discount Account          : 4009

                    Retained Profit & Loss Account : 3200
                    Mispostings Account            : 9999
                    Bad Debt Write Off Account     : 8100
                    Depreciation Account           : 8000
                    Prepayments Account            : 1103
                    Accruals Account               : 2109

 F1 Help F2 Calc F4 QckRef F8 ClrFld
```

The Control Account menu lets you alter the codes for the Control Accounts.

To alter the code, move the cursor to the account number, type in the new number you want to allocate to the control account and **return**. Please note that the number allocated must exist, i.e. you must have set it up within the Nominal Account Structure.

Global Changes

You can make global changes to each of the following:

Ledger Files

You can make changes to:
Sales Turnover
Sales Credit Limit
Purchase Turnover
Purchase Credit Limit
Nominal Budgets

You will be presented with a new screen and on choosing any one of these options you will be asked to enter a percentage change figure.

After entering the figure you will be asked for the (upper and lower) account references you wish to alter. You will then be presented with a warning screen (the text will alter slightly depending upon the option chosen within the original screen). Please note that the change is NOT reversible.

Stock Files

The options to globally change within this are:

Sales Price
Purchase Price
Re-order Level
Re-order Quantity
Discount A
Discount B
Discount C

Payroll Files

Within this option you can alter:

Tax Codes
NI Categories
Payment Rates

The screen for Tax Codes is shown below:

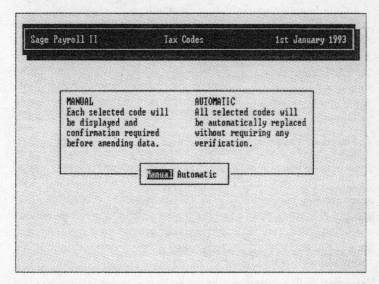

If you choose Manual or Automatic the screen alters to the following (the difference between Automatic and Manual affects the process further on where Manual allows you to confirm the changes to the employees. Manual is the better option for most purposes as you have more control over the process).

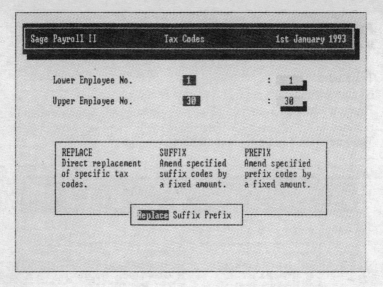

Lower Employee No. **1**   : 1

Upper Employee No. **30**   : 30

REPLACE	SUFFIX	PREFIX
Direct replacement of specific tax codes.	Amend specified suffix codes by a fixed amount.	Amend specified prefix codes by a fixed amount.

Replace Suffix Prefix

You need to enter the upper and lower employee numbers and then choose to:

Replace
Suffix
Prefix

What each of these does is explained on the screen.

You then follow through the remaining screens which are self-explanatory.

The other options follow a similar pattern where you are asked for the original data and then for the changes to this data.

Posting Error Corrections

There are two possibilities here:

Reverse Posting

You are asked for the transaction number you want to reverse (you can use the Audit Trail to find it). The program will then display details of the transaction on the screen and explain the method to reverse the entry (some of the explanations can be interesting !).

Please note that this cancels out the original.

Correct Posting

When you choose this option you are again asked for the transaction number and the details are shown on the screen. You can then alter (some of) the data (remember to **return** to ensure the new data is accepted by the program).

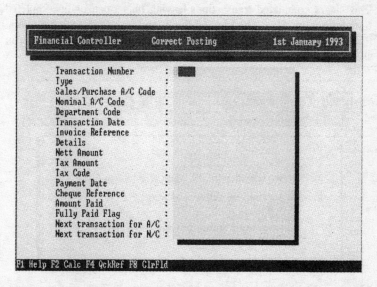

Because of the nature of the data and its security, you may not be able to alter the specific fields you want and may have to find another method of altering the transaction (e.g. cancel cheque or reverse posting).

Incomplete Transactions

This option (which is new to version 5) produces reports of incomplete transactions. The options available are:

Order Processing
Invoicing
Sales Ledger
Purchase Ledger

Within each of these there are several options available and you can use them to produce reports.

Data File Changes

Within this are four options:

Reconfiguration

This clears completed transactions leaving only open or uncompleted transactions on file. The idea of this is to clear space for new data. Please note the warning screen (shown below) which will appear, you should follow the instructions.

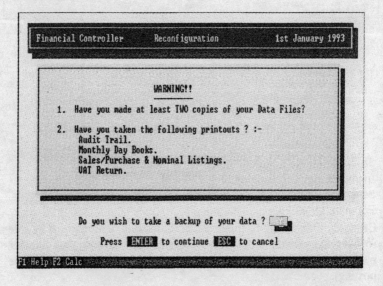

Rebuild Data Files

This option rebuilds the files or creates a new set of empty files depending upon whether you have existing data you wish to use.

This is called Resize data files within v.4 and you can alter the size of your data files as your organisation may have expanded to the extent that you need more Sales Ledger accounts for your customers (e.g. you have more customers than you initially set up SAGE to deal with). This option lets you increase the number of accounts in any of the ledgers.

If you find you have allocated too many accounts in any of the ledgers then you may want to reduce the number (this may make the program work faster and will certainly save space on the disk).

The screen explains the procedure (again it is best to backup your files before doing this).

You will be asked if you have any data (well you either have or you haven't) and whether you want the default nominal codes (if you want to set up your own then please do, however for most purposes the default set is acceptable and you can always delete the ones you do not want).

Compress Data Files

This saves space by taking out deleted records in any of the files, thus making the file smaller.

You can compress any or all of the following files:

Stock Files
Invoice Files
Sales Order Files
Purchase Order Files

Whichever you choose, the screen will explain the procedures.

Payroll Records

You can do four things within this menu option:

P11 Deduction Card / Tax and NI Codes

Within both of these options you will be asked for the lower / upper employee numbers, you will then be able to alter (certain) data.

Reset Check Dates

The purpose of this is to allow you to reset the date if the file has been corrupted or if you have been using test data.

When you select this option you will be asked for the Lower and Upper Employee No. you want to reset the Check Dates for and whether you want the process to be Manual or Automatic.

Record Relocation

This has the purpose of moving the chosen employee records to the front of the data file (otherwise there will be empty records interleaved with live ones where employees have left or died). This will make processing quicker. You can also use this option to relocate an employee within the pay records.

Data Verification

SAGE can be used to check that the data is acceptable (i.e. that no errors exist). The types of error that may be picked up by this part of the program are:

Input errors	Data that is outside of the values expected.
Internal inconsistencies	Where data is inconsistent with itself.
Corrupt data	Usually caused by disk problems.
Missing files	
Incorrect file sizes	

There are two options:

Account Data
You will be asked three questions:

Validate Data Only
Correct Data Automatically
Display, Printer or File

After answering these a report will appear which will (hopefully) display the message NO ERRORS FOUND. If there is a problem the program may display a message on screen telling you how to solve the problem, it is then merely a matter of doing as it says. The actual manual that comes with the program gives a very complete listing of the various error messages and their solution.

If you are confused and the program has displayed error messages you can ask your supplier for more help or ring the SAGE Help line. It might be wise to request expert help rather than make the problem worse by fiddling without knowing exactly what you are doing.

If you do decide to fiddle then **PLEASE** backup your data onto a new set of floppy discs (and mark them as such) before doing so, then if you do mess thing up you can restore your files.

It is worth running this program several times to clear all the problems as they can be related and one pass may not clear them all. The program is called DISK DOCTOR and can be run outside of the menu (see below).

Important
If you back up your files regularly and keep several versions then even if there is a problem the data can easily be restored.

Disk Doctor options can be run from the DOS prompt by typing DOCTOR
followed by various switches (the dash is necessary)
-v   validates the data
-c   automatically corrects
-p   prints an error listing
-f   sends the error listing to a file

File Import

You can import data directly from other applications into SAGE files (the data files will have an extension of **DTA**) by using this option. The original files must be in **CSV** format (comma separated values).

CSV format

In this format each record in the file in on a separate line and each field within the record is separated by a comma. You can create CSV files using a text editor if you wish.

The SAGE manual has specific details on how to carry out this procedure, the screen below gives the various options available.

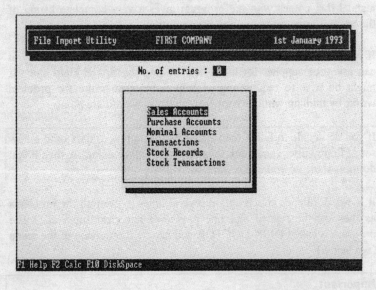

Backup Utilities

This part of the Utilities menu is of great importance, you should backup your data **very** frequently (with luck you will not need to restore the data).

When you choose this option, you will be asked next whether you want to:

Backup Data Files
or
Restore Data Files

Backup Data Files

There is rather a difference between Backup and Restore, Backup copies the data files **from** the hard disc onto the floppy disc being used as a backup.

The reason to backup your files is to be able to restore the files if the originals on the hard disc are corrupted or perhaps deleted by accident. Normally this should not occur but experience suggests that it might (usually to people who do not take care of their files by backing up).

You should backup regularly, at least at the end of every day and possibly more often if you are entering much data. The time spend backing up is minimal compared with the chaos and loss of business that can be caused by not being able to restore the files.

Always
*   write protect your backup discs after use
*   write the details on the disc label
*   keep them somewhere very safe
*   keep at least three sets of backup discs (if you backup daily this means the last three days' sets). Personally I would also create and keep weekly sets since it may take some time for you to become aware that some of your files are corrupt.

Restore Data Files

Restore copies the files from the floppy disc **to** the hard disc (writing over any data files that already exist on the hard disc).

If you mistakenly restore instead of backing up you will write over your existing data files on the hard disc with older copies thus wasting many hours of work!

The screens for Backup and Restore are similar, once you have selected either then you will be asked whether you want to deal with the Accounts Data Files or the Payroll Data Files. Choose one of these and you will see a screen as shown below.

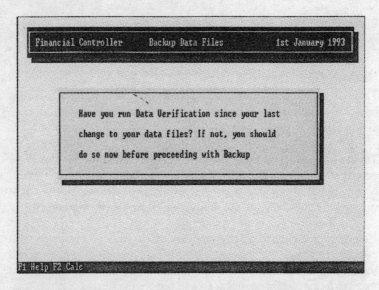

Then the following screen will appear:

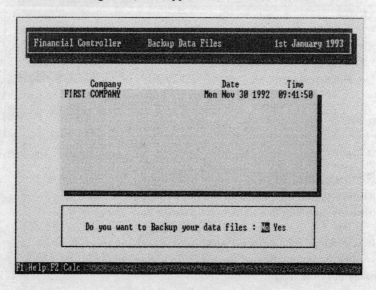

The data shown on the screen itemises the recent backups you have made in order. If you choose **Yes** to backing up your files the screen will alter slightly and suggest the drive to backup to (normally this will be **A**, the first or only floppy drive).

If you want to backup to another drive then type the letter for the drive (e.g. B) and the data will be backed up onto this drive instead.

Place a floppy disc in the drive **before** returning or typing another drive letter and you will then see the following message appear on the bottom of the screen:

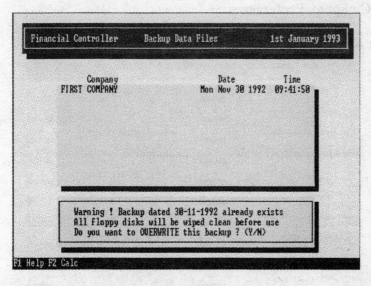

You need to answer the question and then messages appear in the box telling you the process is taking place.

When the operation has been finished, the menu will reappear and you can **ESC** back to whichever menu level you want.

Defaults

You are able to choose various settings within the SAGE program (v.5 only) by using this option (with previous versions you had to use the Install program). You have four choices:

Company Preferences
Drive Letters
Printer Setup
Periscope Setup

Company Preferences

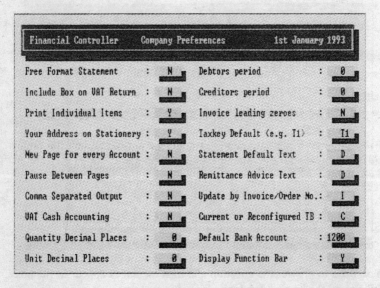

Financial Controller	Company Preferences	1st January 1993	
Free Format Statement	: N	Debtors period	: 0
Include Box on VAT Return	: N	Creditors period	: 0
Print Individual Items	: Y	Invoice leading zeroes	: N
Your Address on Stationery	: Y	Taxkey Default (e.g. T1)	: T1
New Page for every Account	: N	Statement Default Text	: D
Pause Between Pages	: N	Remittance Advice Text	: D
Comma Separated Output	: N	Update by Invoice/Order No.:	I
VAT Cash Accounting	: N	Current or Reconfigured TB	: C
Quantity Decimal Places	: 0	Default Bank Account	: 1200
Unit Decimal Places	: 0	Display Function Bar	: Y

Options that you are likely to want to change are:

VAT Cash Accounting (if this is the way you want to account for VAT)
Debtors and Creditors periods
Quantity Decimal Places

When you have finished making the changes **ESC** and you will be asked whether you want to save the changes you have made.

Drive Letters

Here you can alter the disk drive you are using to store the data (obviously you have to have more than one drive to do so).

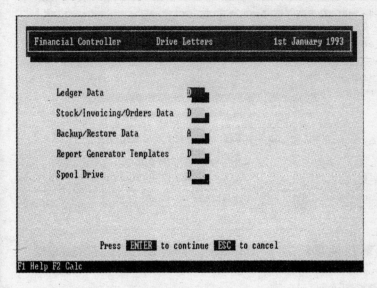

If you only have one hard drive (or only one partition) then the drive will be **C** (except for the Backup / Restore option).

Printer Setup

This screen lets you add, delete or change your printer.

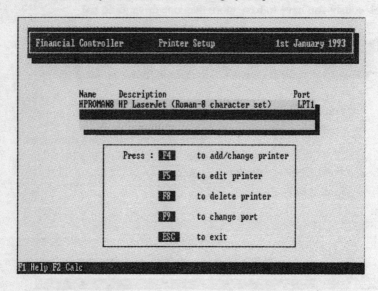

```
Financial Controller      Printer Setup        1st January 1993


    Name      Description                           Port
    HPROMAN8  HP LaserJet (Roman-8 character set)    LPT1


            Press : F4    to add/change printer

                    F5    to edit printer

                    F8    to delete printer

                    F9    to change port

                    ESC   to exit

F1 Help F2 Calc
```

Periscope Setup

If you are using WINDOWS or any other program that already uses
the key combination of **ALT return**, then you will need to change this
setting. You can only change the second key (the **return**) key and the
alternative keys are given in the SAGE Installation Manual (Appendix
2.1).

Once the screen is shown, you have to select the line you want to alter
and then enter the changes. When you have entered the changes just
ESC and follow the prompts on-screen to finish.

Details of how to change this for previous versions are in the
appendices.

APPENDIX ONE

Multi Companies
If your organisation consists of more than one company then you need to set up SAGE to deal with this. You can have up to ten different companies within the program.

Setting up different companies
There are two methods of achieving this, but whichever way you choose, the initial screen should list all the companies you have set up as shown in the example below:

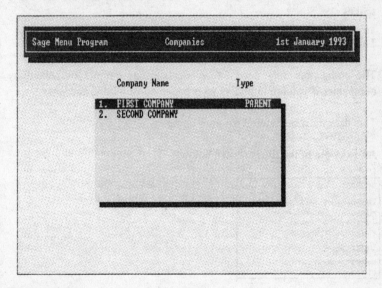

Automatically
Run a program called **MULTICO** which is available from SAGE (if it was not included with the program).

Manually
This should only be attempted if you have a good grasp of DOS and of the mechanics of sub directories.

Details of the companies needs to be entered into a file called **COMPANY** (there is no extension) which is held in the SAGE directory. You can edit this file by using any text editor.

The data to be entered into the COMPANY file (for each company) is as follows:

```
Type          (Parent or Subsidiary)
Name
Address 1
Address 2
Address 3
Address 4
```

The name needs to be enclosed in inverted commas if it contains any spaces.

There can only be one parent company.

The companies only need to be identified as parents or subsidiary companies if you are intending to produce consolidated accounts.

This data must be entered for each company.

An example of the file is shown below:

```
parent
name "first company"
address1 "1 The Square"
address2 "Newtown"
address3 "Cornwall"
address4 "TR5 6RD"

subsidiary
name "second company"
etc
```

The file is held in the SAGE directory e.g. C:\SAGE

Once you have entered the names you need to save the file and then to create the sub directory structure for the new company and then copy **empty** SAGE data files into these directories.

It is obviously important to have a disc with the directory structure and files ready for this purpose.

The directory structure should look like this (you can use the **DOS tree** command to check).

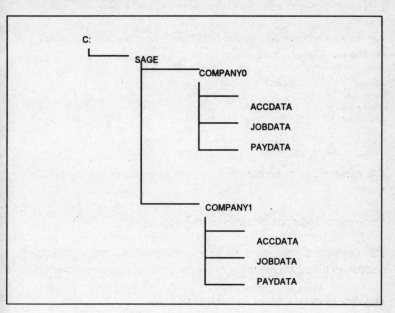

APPENDIX TWO

The Periscope

This is a useful utility that lets you look at the data held within your SAGE files (whatever program you are actually using at the time, for example you could be word-processing a letter to a client and want to look at how much the client owes to you).

To use the periscope, you first need to install it into memory (it is a TSR and stays in memory until called upon) to do this type **VIEW** from the DOS prompt (possibly you will first have to move to the SAGE directory, e.g. C:\SAGE) and **return** and then you can call up the periscope screen by pressing **ALT** and **return**.

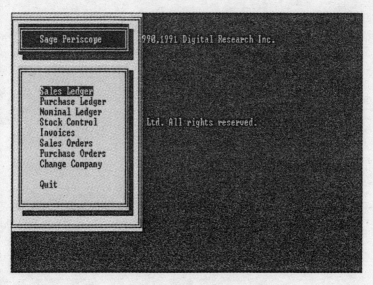

Please note that the hot-key combination of **ALT** and **return** cannot be used within WINDOWS and you will need to alter the combination if you are running SAGE from within WINDOWS.

The previous screen shows the various options within Periscope and the keys below can be used within it to display the data:

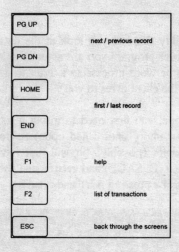

PG UP	
	next / previous record
PG DN	
HOME	
	first / last record
END	
F1	help
F2	list of transactions
ESC	back through the screens

APPENDIX THREE

Altering the Password

It would be sensible to alter the original password and possibly to increase the number of passwords so that each member of staff using SAGE has their own. When using passwords to protect the system there are several guidelines for their most effective use and these are outlined below.

To be effective passwords have to work. They should:

* Be unique to each user.
* Not easily guessed (wife's name, dog's name, initials).
* Changed regularly.
* Not written down.
* Not given to anyone else (**for any reason**).

Unfortunately the research that has been carried out shows that most passwords are far too easy to find out or guess and users tend to treat them as a kind of joke.

To alter or add to passwords involves running a special program from the DOS prompt called **installs**. You have to run the program from the installation discs to alter the password by typing

A:INSTALLS PASSWORD.EXE

this copies the password program onto your hard disc, the syntax of the command is shown below.

ALWAYS delete it from the hard drive (otherwise users can change the password at will), you will be given the option to do this (as shown on the screen below).

---

v4 of SAGE allows you to copy the file onto your hard drive and then leave it there, this is not a good move, always run it from the floppy. With version 4 you have to type
A:Password
(you must have the original disc in the drive)

```
[DR DOS] D:\SAGE5>a:installs password.exe

PKSFX (R)  FAST!  Self Extract Utility  Version 1.01  07-21-89
Copyright 1989 PKWARE Inc.  All Rights Reserved.
PKSFX Reg. U.S. Pat. and Tm. Off.

Searching EXE: A:/INSTALLS.EXE
  Exploding: PASSWORD.EXE

[DR DOS] D:\SAGE5>password aa wonder all

    WONDER    :  SP  SR  PP  PR  NP  NR  MR  ST  SO  PO  IV  UT

Do you want to delete the file D:\SAGE5\PASSWORD.EXE ? (Y/N)

Password program file deleted

[DR DOS] D:\SAGE5>_
```

The command to be entered could be (no spaces between the type and
option):

PASSWORD AA WONDER ALL

This would add a password called WONDER to all the accounting
menus.

The parameters you can use are as follows:

PASSWORD type option password menus (there is no space
between type and option)

type
A   accounts
P   payroll

option
A   add a password
D   delete a password
V   view passwords

password
The actual password you want to use (up to 10 characters).

menus

The menus you want the password to apply to (you can obviously set different passwords to different parts of the program):

SP	sales ledger postings	IV	invoice production
SR	sales ledger reports	UT	utilities
PP	purchase ledger postings	ALL	all menus
PR	purchase ledger reports	ED	employee details
NP	nominal ledger postings	PP	process payroll
NR	nominal ledger reports	SS	statutory sick pay
MR	management reports	SM	statutory maternity pay
ST	stock control	GP	government parameters
SO	sales order processing	CD	company details
PO	purchase order processing	RG	report generator

Please change your passwords regularly **and** delete the original password LETMEIN from the system as it is widely known.

APPENDIX FOUR

Changing the way SAGE is configured (v5)

Once you have installed the program, you can alter some of the pre-defined settings. You are able to do this through the **SAGESET** program which can be run from the DOS prompt by typing the word **SAGESET** followed by **return**.

It would be unwise to alter any setting unless you are sure that you want to and that the end result will be satisfactory.

Always note down the original settings **before** altering them so that they can be re-set if necessary.

Complete details of each and every option is given in the SAGE installation manual.

The SAGE set screen gives the following options (some of which are also available within the Utilities Defaults option):

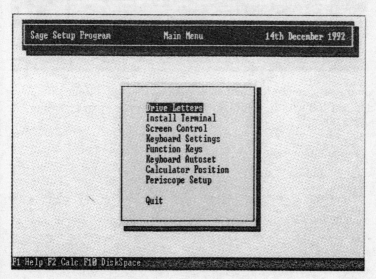

Versions 4 (of SAGE) and Below

The following refers only to v.4 and below

Once you have installed the program, you can alter some of the pre-defined settings. You are able to do this through the **Install** program which can be run from the DOS prompt by typing the word **INSTALL** followed by **return**.

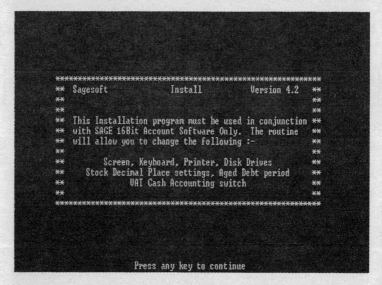

On the next screen, the first three options allow you to install new or different settings, the fourth to change the way the program works.

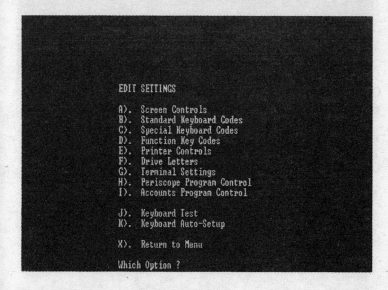

```
SAGE SOFTWARE INSTALLATION ROUTINE

A).  Install Terminal
B).  Install Printer
C).  Install Drive Letters
D).  Edit settings

Q).  Abandon the program
X).  Exit from program

Which Option ?
```

If you choose **D** then the following screen appears:

```
EDIT SETTINGS

A).  Screen Controls
B).  Standard Keyboard Codes
C).  Special Keyboard Codes
D).  Function Key Codes
E).  Printer Controls
F).  Drive Letters
G).  Terminal Settings
H).  Periscope Program Control
I).  Accounts Program Control

J).  Keyboard Test
K).  Keyboard Auto-Setup

X).  Return to Menu

Which Option ?
```

The options follow a fairly standard layout and method of alteration, the following are examples of the ones you are most likely to want to alter:

The Periscope Settings
If you are using WINDOWS or any other program that already uses
the key combination of **ALT return**, then you will need to change this
setting. You can only change the second key (the **return**) key and the
alternative keys are given in the SAGE installation manual.

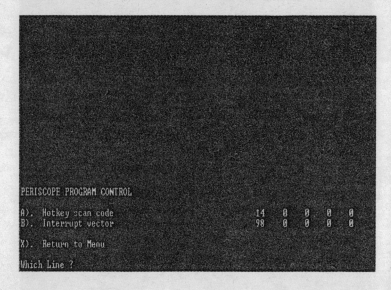

```
PERISCOPE PROGRAM CONTROL

A).  Hotkey scan code                    14    0    0    0    0
B).  Interrupt vector                    98    0    0    0    0

X).  Return to Menu

Which Line ?
```

Once the screen is shown, you have to select the line you want to alter
and then enter the changes (an example appears opposite).

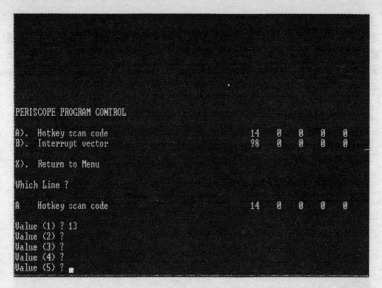

```
PERISCOPE PROGRAM CONTROL

A).  Hotkey scan code                          14    0    0    0    0
B).  Interrupt vector                          98    0    0    0    0

X).  Return to Menu

Which Line ?

A    Hotkey scan code                          14    0    0    0    0

Value (1) ? 13
Value (2) ?
Value (3) ?
Value (4) ?
Value (5) ?
```

When you have entered the changes just follow the prompts on-screen
to finish.

Account Program Control

The one that you are most likely to want to change is **C**, the number of days used in the calculation of aged debtors and creditors lists. The first value is the debtors period (30 days, 60 days, 90 days and older), the second the purchase period.

```
ACCOUNTS PROGRAM CONTROL

A).  VAT Cash Accounting                        0    0    0    0    0
B).  Qty D.P / Unit D.P                          2    2    0    0    0
C).  Debtors period / Creditors period         30   30    0    0    0
D).  Invoice leading zeroes                      0    0    0    0    0
E).  Statement Default Text [D=0,G=1,I=2]        0    0    0    0    0
F).  Remittance Advice Text [D=0,I=1]            0    0    0    0    0
G).  Update with Invoice/Order No.[I=0,O=1]      0    0    0    0    0

X).  Return to Menu

Which Line ?
```

Printer Controls

This lets you customise the way your printer deals with the various forms and reports that SAGE generates.

You can alter these to fit the paper you use, you may need to experiment a little (remember to write down the original settings **before** you change them). Full details of the settings are given in the SAGE installation manual.

APPENDIX FIVE

Converting Data Files from Previous Versions of SAGE

A utility called MINDEX comes with the program and this converts the data files for use with version 5.

Please note that using this program under certain circumstances may reboot your computer and it may be necessary to have the conversion carried out by the firm selling you version 5 if this happens.

Backup your files **twice** before attempting the conversion.

APPENDIX SIX

Versions of the SAGE Program

You can buy the following different versions of SAGE and you can easily upgrade from one to another:

SAGE Bookkeeper
This is the simplest version and consists of:
Sales ledger
Purchase ledger
Nominal ledger
plus you can produce a trial balance and profit and loss account.

SAGE Accountant
This adds the following to the Bookkeeper program:
Balance sheets
Budgetary control
Credit control facilities (inc. statements and debt chasing letters)
Password control
Year to Date turnover figures
Recurring Bank Payments (e.g. Standing Orders) and journal entries
Depreciation
Prepayments and Accruals
Writing off bad debts.

Accountant Plus
This includes (as well as the above)
Stock control and the production of invoices automatically from the stock files (with automatic updating of the sales and nominal ledger accounts and of the stock account).

Financial Controller
This is the totally integrated version (of the above) and includes additional features such as:
Order processing
Inventory management and accounting.

INDEX

A

account code, 9, 13, 16, 18, 20, 44, 50, 51
account names, 16
account reference, 11, 16, 20, 24, 38, 123
accruals, 13, 46, 47, 136, 173
address list, 23
asset, 4, 48, 49, 54
audit trail, 14, 34, 38, 47, 49, 129, 143

B

backing up files, 53, 104, 145, 147, 148, 149, 150, 151
bad debts, 14, 15, 38, 54, 173
Balance Sheet, 4, 14, 15, 17, 18, 50, 53, 129
bank, 13, 14, 15, 41, 42, 43, 45, 50, 51, 72, 129, 132, 173
batched data entry, 19, 21, 25
bounced cheque, 35
budget, 17, 54

C

cancel cheque, 34, 35, 143
cash payment, 43, 51 129
cash receipt, 43, 51, 129
categories, 4, 66, 78, 82, 107, 108, 109, 113, 141
cheque, 32, 33, 34, 35, 42, 43
cheques, 79, 81, 92, 102, 103, 132, 143
consolidation, 50
contras, 36
control account, 13, 21, 52, 55, 139, 140
credit limit, 12, 123
credit notes, 19, 25, 29, 129
customer details, 10, 11, 23, 27

D

day books, 33, 51
debtors (aged), 25, 170
delete, 4, 13, 17, 31, 46, 49, 112, 119, 126, 132, 135, 145, 154, 161, 163
department, 20, 42, 44, 75, 83, 110, 123, 130
depreciation, 13, 14, 15, 48, 49, 50, 54, 136, 173
discount, 12, 110, 123, 129, 140
DOS, 4, 126, 127, 132, 134, 135, 147, 155, 157, 159, 161, 165, 166

E

enquiries, 4, 118
errors, 26, 33, 35, 143, 146, 147

If you would like a complete catalogue of our entire range of Radio, Electronics and Computer Books then please send a Stamped Addressed Envelope to:

BERNARD BABANI (publishing) LTD
THE GRAMPIANS
SHEPHERDS BUSH ROAD
LONDON W6 7NF
ENGLAND